SCHOLASTIC

2025
BOOK OF WORLD RECORDS

BY
MICHAEL BRIGHT
CHRIS HAWKES
ABIGAIL MITCHELL
CYNTHIA O'BRIEN
MIKE ROBBINS
DONALD SOMMERVILLE
ANTONIA VAN DER MEER

Copyright © 2024 by Scholastic Inc.

All rights reserved. Published by Scholastic Inc., *Publishers since 1920.* SCHOLASTIC and associated logos are trademarks and/or registered trademarks of Scholastic Inc.

Due to this book's publication date, the majority of statistics are current as of February 2024. The publisher does not have any control over and does not assume any responsibility for author or third-party websites or their content.

No part of this publication may be reproduced, stored in a retrieval system, or transmitted in any form or by any means, electronic, mechanical, photocopying, recording, or otherwise, without written permission of the publisher. For information regarding permission, write to Scholastic Inc., Attention: Permissions Department, 557 Broadway, New York, NY 10012.

This book was created and produced by Toucan Books Limited.
Text: Michael Bright, Chris Hawkes, Abigail Mitchell, Cynthia O'Brien, Mike Robbins, Donald Sommerville, Antonia van der Meer
Designer: Lee Riches
Editor: Anna Southgate
Proofreader: Marilyn Knowlton
Index: Marie Lorimer
Toucan would like to thank Cian O'Day for picture research.

ISBN 978-1-5461-2271-5

10 9 8 7 6 5 4 3 2 1   24 25 26 27 28

Printed in the U.S.A.   40

First printing, 2024

CONTENTS

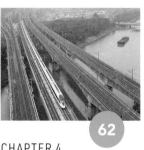

music makers trending

KEN AT THE OSCARS Wearing a pink, gem-studded suit, cowboy hat, and shades, actor Ryan Gosling took to the stage during the 2024 Oscars for a unique performance of "I'm Just Ken," his hit song from the movie *Barbie*. The Kenergy flowed as Gosling was joined on stage by his fellow movie Kens, plus sixty-two more dancing Kens. The number culminated in an impressive solo by legendary Guns N' Roses guitarist Slash.

FIFTIETH ANNIVERSARY OF HIP-HOP The music genre hip-hop celebrated its fiftieth anniversary in 2023. Its origins go back to a party thrown in the community room of a Bronx, New York, apartment building in 1973 by teenager Cindy Campbell and her brother, Clive, also known as DJ Kool Herc. Hip-hop's 2023 birthday celebrations included a spectacular Grammys concert segment in December featuring some of the genre's greats—from DJ Jazzy Jeff & the Fresh Prince to Queen Latifah.

AI GENERATES A HIT "Heart on My Sleeve," a new song with vocals that sounded like Drake's and The Weeknd's, went viral in April 2023 with 15 million views on TikTok and hundreds of thousands of streams on other platforms. The only catch was that Drake and The Weeknd had never heard of the song! It was the creation of TikTok user Ghostwriter977, who wrote and produced the song using artificial intelligence to fake the voices of its "stars." After just two days of streaming, Universal Music Group forced the song to be taken down.

SEISMIC ACTIVITY AT THE ERAS TOUR The year 2023 saw Taylor Swift make the news for several reasons, the most bizarre of which was seismic activity! The artist spent much of 2023 on her blockbuster Eras Tour, performing two shows in Seattle in July. Dancing Swifties in the crowd (along with the concert's sound system) generated so much movement that a nearby seismometer registered the shaking in the ground as equivalent to that of a small earthquake, with a 2.3 magnitude! The "Swift Quake," as it was named, seemed to match up with big moments in Swift's set list in both shows.

THE BEATLES' LAST RELEASE Only two of The Beatles were still alive in 2023, yet the iconic British band released a new track featuring all four original members. "Now and Then" was on a demo recorded by songwriter John Lennon before he was killed in 1980. In 2023, aided by AI technology, producers isolated Lennon's voice on the cassette tape and combined it with new parts from Paul McCartney and Ringo Starr, and a guitar part recorded by the late George Harrison in the 1990s.

MOST-STREAMED SONG OF 2023
"FLOWERS"
MILEY CYRUS

Miley Cyrus's catchy "Flowers" was the most-streamed song of 2023, with more than 1.6 billion plays on Spotify. Released in January, the song spent eight weeks at the top of the *Billboard* 100 chart and broke records with more than 100 million streams in a single week. Cowriter Michael Pollack called the song a "unicorn" for its amazing success, but it might surprise fans to learn that the song was originally written as a slow piano ballad before it was revised into its final peppy form. "Flowers" appears on Cyrus's eighth studio album, *Endless Summer Vacation*, and was named one of Spotify's top 10 songs of the summer—the no. 1 being Eslabon Armado and Peso Pluma's "Ella Baila Sola."

MOST-STREAMED SONGS OF 2023

"Flowers," Miley Cyrus

"Kill Bill," SZA

"As It Was," Harry Styles

"Seven," Jung Kook ft. Latto

"Ella Baila Sola," Eslabon Armado and Peso Pluma

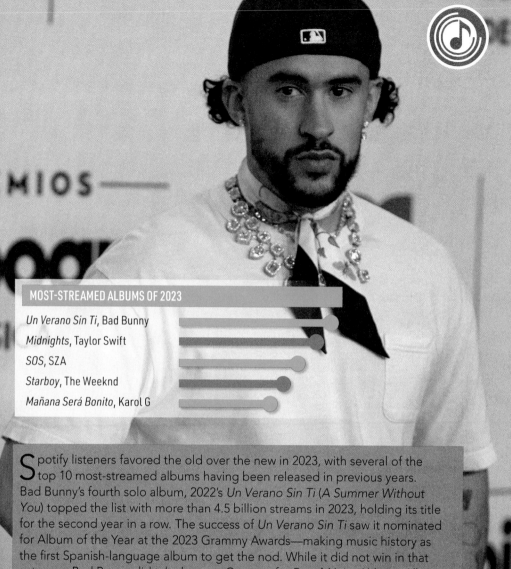

MOST-STREAMED ALBUMS OF 2023

Un Verano Sin Ti, Bad Bunny

Midnights, Taylor Swift

SOS, SZA

Starboy, The Weeknd

Mañana Será Bonito, Karol G

Spotify listeners favored the old over the new in 2023, with several of the top 10 most-streamed albums having been released in previous years. Bad Bunny's fourth solo album, 2022's *Un Verano Sin Ti* (*A Summer Without You*) topped the list with more than 4.5 billion streams in 2023, holding its title for the second year in a row. The success of *Un Verano Sin Ti* saw it nominated for Album of the Year at the 2023 Grammy Awards—making music history as the first Spanish-language album to get the nod. While it did not win in that category, Bad Bunny did take home a Grammy for Best Música Urbana Album (an award for Latin albums).

MOST-STREAMED ALBUM OF 2023
UN VERANO SIN TI
BAD BUNNY

MOST-LIKED VIDEO ON YOUTUBE
"DESPACITO"

Hitting 52 million likes in December 2023, "Despacito" remains the most-liked video on YouTube. The Puerto Rican dance track by Luis Fonsi, which features Daddy Yankee, came out in 2017 and took only six months to become the most-streamed song in history. It's no surprise that it also became the first music video to notch up four, five, six, and seven billion views on YouTube, before hitting eight billion in November 2022. That's not to say it's everybody's favorite. According to YouTube's stats, the video is also in the top 20 most-disliked videos on the platform, with more than five million dislikes before YouTube made them invisible.

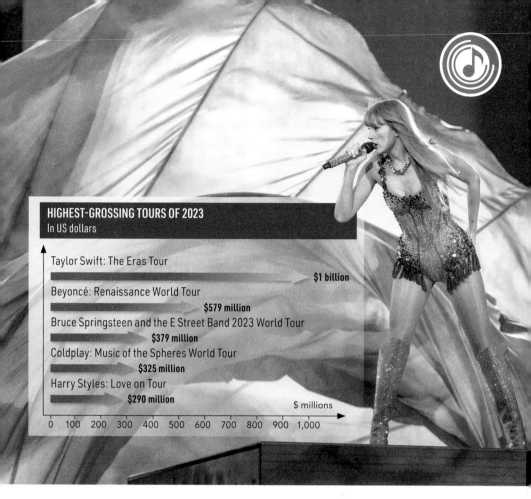

HIGHEST-GROSSING TOURS OF 2023
In US dollars

Taylor Swift: The Eras Tour — $1 billion

Beyoncé: Renaissance World Tour — $579 million

Bruce Springsteen and the E Street Band 2023 World Tour — $379 million

Coldplay: Music of the Spheres World Tour — $325 million

Harry Styles: Love on Tour — $290 million

$ millions

0 100 200 300 400 500 600 700 800 900 1,000

HIGHEST-GROSSING TOUR
TAYLOR SWIFT: THE ERAS TOUR

Swifties around the world rejoiced in 2023 when Taylor Swift brought her most exciting show yet to the stadium stage. Taylor Swift: The Eras Tour is more than a three-hour-long performance, featuring songs from all ten of Swift's studio albums. As her legendary legion of fans rushed to put on their friendship bracelets, it is no wonder that Swift's show was the highest-grossing tour of the year, making $1 billion. Swift's show famously crashed ticketing websites, but unlucky fans who could not see it live were given a chance to be a part of the magic with *Taylor Swift: The Eras Tour* concert movie, released in October 2023. It swiftly became the top-grossing concert film ever released!

FIRST RAPPER TO TOP *BILLBOARD* HOT 100 CHART

DRAKE

Drake released his album *If You're Reading This It's Too Late* through iTunes on February 12, 2015. The digital album sold 495,000 units in its first week and entered the *Billboard* 200 at no. 1, making Drake the first rap artist ever to top the chart. The album also helped Drake secure another record: most hits on the *Billboard* Hot 100 at one time. On March 7, 2015, Drake had fourteen hit songs on the chart, matching the record the Beatles have held since 1964. Since releasing his first hit single, "Best I Ever Had," in 2009, Drake has seen many of his singles go multiplatinum, including "Hotline Bling," which sold 41,000 copies in its first week and had eighteen weeks at no.1 on the *Billboard* Hot 100.

TOP GROUP/DUO

FUERZA REGIDA

The 2023 *Billboard* Music Award for Top Duo/Group went to Fuerza Regida, in a big win for Mexican music in the US. The band made waves in 2023 with "Bebe Dame," their collaboration with fellow nominees Grupo Frontera, and also released tracks with Becky G, Shakira, and rapper Myke Towers. While 2023 marks their first win in this category, Fuerza Regida have been making music since 2015, and released their eighth studio album in 2023. The BBMAs featured a diverse group of other nominees, from K-Pop girl group Fifty Fifty to Latin group Eslabon Armado to heavy metal icons Metallica.

TOP-SELLING RECORDING GROUP
THE BEATLES

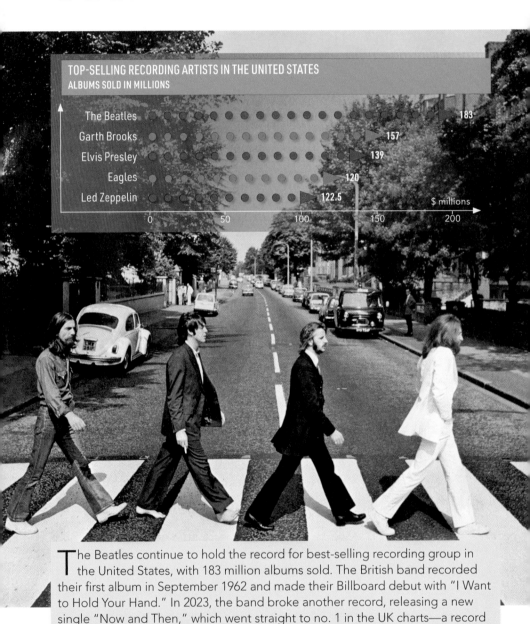

TOP-SELLING RECORDING ARTISTS IN THE UNITED STATES
ALBUMS SOLD IN MILLIONS

Artist	$ millions
The Beatles	183
Garth Brooks	157
Elvis Presley	139
Eagles	120
Led Zeppelin	122.5

0   50   100   150   200 $ millions

The Beatles continue to hold the record for best-selling recording group in the United States, with 183 million albums sold. The British band recorded their first album in September 1962 and made their Billboard debut with "I Want to Hold Your Hand." In 2023, the band broke another record, releasing a new single "Now and Then," which went straight to no. 1 in the UK charts—a record fifty-four years since their last no. 1 hit in that country.

Twenty One Pilots collaborated with their fans in 2020 to create the longest music video ever! The official video for their hit "Level of Concern" lasted 177 days, 16 hours, 10 minutes, and 25 seconds, with the song constantly looping as fan-made video submissions were played on the live stream. The band announced the end of its "never-ending" stream by joking that the only way it would stop was for the power to go out . . . followed by a video of band member Joshua Dun overloading his Christmas tree with lights!

LONGEST-EVER MUSIC VIDEO
"LEVEL OF CONCERN" TWENTY ONE PILOTS

RICHEST FEMALE SINGER
RIHANNA

Officially naming Robyn "Rihanna" Fenty a billionaire in 2022, *Forbes* certified the Barbadian icon as the richest female singer in the world. Her estimated $1.4 billion net worth doesn't just come from her eight studio albums—the majority comes from her Fenty Beauty makeup line. With a diverse range of shades for all skin tones and a commitment to cruelty-free production, Rihanna's cosmetics line is a real hit, outshining many other celebrity contributions to the industry.

LONGEST-RUNNING NO. 1 SINGLE "OLD TOWN ROAD"

From March through July 2019, rapper Lil Nas X's "Old Town Road" spent seventeen weeks in the no. 1 spot, pushing past "Despacito" from Luis Fonsi and Mariah Carey's "One Sweet Day," each of which spent sixteen weeks at the top of the charts. Lil Nas X's real name is Montero Hill, and he is from Atlanta, Georgia. He recorded the song himself, and people first fell in love with the catchy tune on TikTok. "Old Town Road" made it to the country charts, but it was later dropped for not being considered a country song. Disagreements about its genre only fueled interest in the song, however, and it subsequently hit no. 1. The song was then remixed and rerecorded with country music star Billy Ray Cyrus, whose wife at the time, Tish, encouraged him to become involved.

ACT WITH THE MOST COUNTRY MUSIC AWARDS IN ONE NIGHT

LAINEY WILSON

Lainey Wilson made country music history in November 2023, when she won five awards at the Country Music Awards. The triumph marked the most awards ever won by a female artist in a single night. The awards were Entertainer of the Year, Female Vocalist of the Year, Album of the Year (for *Bell Bottom Country*), Musical Event of the Year (for her collaboration with HARDY on "wait in the truck"), and Music Video of the Year ("wait in the truck"). Flames lit up the stage behind Wilson as she performed her hit "Wildflowers and Wild Horses" at the ceremony to cap off her big night.

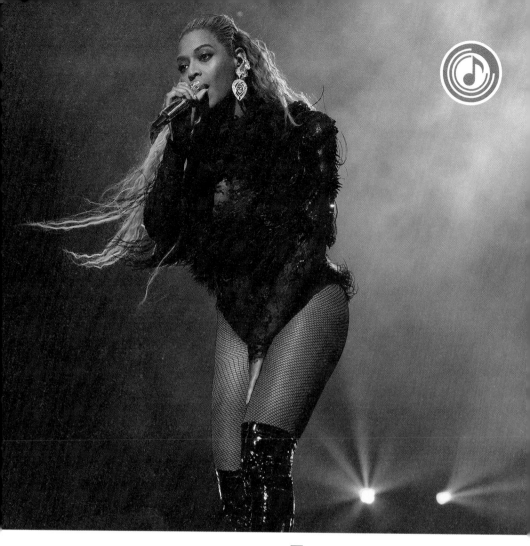

BEYONCÉ

MUSICIAN WITH THE **MOST GRAMMYS**

With thirty-two awards in total, Queen Bey reigns supreme as the musician with the most Grammys of all time. Her most recent wins—four in all—were presented at the 65th Grammy Awards in 2023. Her seventh studio album, *Renaissance*, won Best Dance/Electronic Album, while songs from the album won Best R&B Song ("Cuff It"), Best Traditional R&B Vocal Performance ("Plastic Off the Sofa"), and Best Dance Recording ("Break My Soul"). Both Beyoncé and her husband, Jay-Z, have eighty-eight Grammy nominations, tying them for most-nominated artists of all time.

FIRST ALL-SPANISH ALBUM TO TOP THE *BILLBOARD* 200 CHART

EL ÚLTIMO TOUR DEL MUNDO
BAD BUNNY

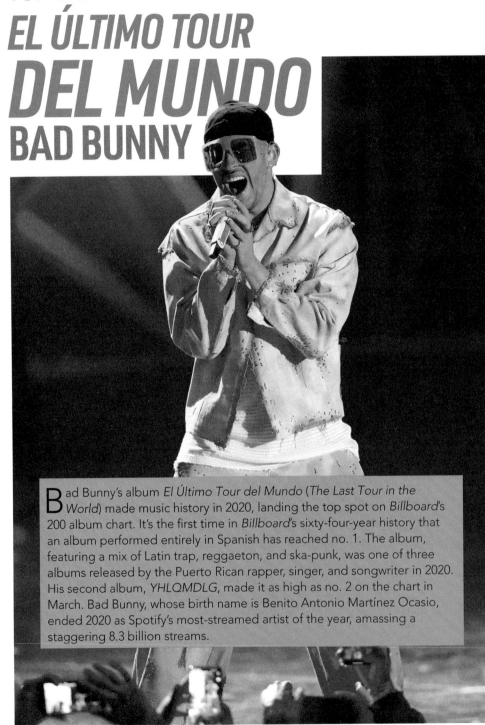

Bad Bunny's album *El Último Tour del Mundo* (*The Last Tour in the World*) made music history in 2020, landing the top spot on *Billboard*'s 200 album chart. It's the first time in *Billboard*'s sixty-four-year history that an album performed entirely in Spanish has reached no. 1. The album, featuring a mix of Latin trap, reggaeton, and ska-punk, was one of three albums released by the Puerto Rican rapper, singer, and songwriter in 2020. His second album, *YHLQMDLG*, made it as high as no. 2 on the chart in March. Bad Bunny, whose birth name is Benito Antonio Martínez Ocasio, ended 2020 as Spotify's most-streamed artist of the year, amassing a staggering 8.3 billion streams.

MOST-AWARDED ARTISTS EVER
TAYLOR SWIFT AND DRAKE

The 2023 *Billboard* Music Awards (BBMAs) left Taylor Swift and Drake neck and neck in the race to become the BBMAs' most-awarded artist ever. Swift won ten awards at the ceremony and Drake won five—numbers that brought them to an impressive total of thirty-nine awards each to date. So mirrored are their successes that both artists have won the Top Artist award three times—Swift in 2013, 2015, and 2023 and Drake in 2017, 2019, and 2022—and the Top *Billboard* 200 Album twice (Swift in 2013 and 2015, Drake in 2017 and 2019). Despite the awards each received in 2023, neither was the winningest act of the night. That honor went to Morgan Wallen, who left the ceremony with a total of eleven awards.

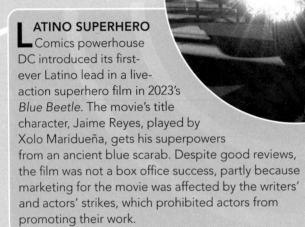

LATINO SUPERHERO

Comics powerhouse DC introduced its first-ever Latino lead in a live-action superhero film in 2023's *Blue Beetle*. The movie's title character, Jaime Reyes, played by Xolo Maridueña, gets his superpowers from an ancient blue scarab. Despite good reviews, the film was not a box office success, partly because marketing for the movie was affected by the writers' and actors' strikes, which prohibited actors from promoting their work.

WRITERS AND ACTORS GO ON STRIKE

Two unions made headlines in 2023 with strikes that saw film and TV production grind to a halt. The Writers Guild of America strike, which began in May, was mainly about pay for residuals (episodes being repeated) on streaming services. It coincided with a strike by Hollywood's biggest union—the Screen Actors Guild-American Federation of Television and Radio Artists, which represents performers—that began in July. The writers' strike ended in September, but the actors' strike dragged on until November.

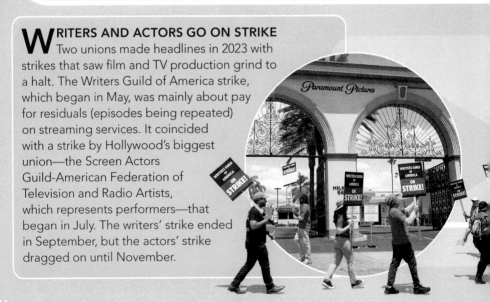

GAMESPOT'S TV SHOW OF THE YEAR

One of gamers' highlights of 2023 was HBO's live-action adaptation of video game developer Naughty Dog's *The Last of Us*, which premiered in January. Starring Pedro Pascal as Joel, a smuggler, and Bella Ramsey as his teenage charge, Ellie, the show brings to life a postapocalyptic world in which a pandemic has turned many into zombielike beings. Gaming website GameSpot named the series its TV show of 2023, calling it the best ever live-action version of a video game.

WAXWORK GOES VIRAL

Wrestler-turned-actor Dwayne "The Rock" Johnson made the news in 2023 after a wax figure unveiled at the Parisian Grévin Museum in October appeared to have a much lighter skin tone than that of the real man, who is half-Black and half-Samoan. After images of the statue went viral, many accused the museum of whitewashing the actor. The Rock addressed the controversy in a video on social media, stating that his team would reach out to the museum for some "improvements."

THE YEAR OF THE CONCERT FILM

More fans than ever were able to watch recorded live performances in 2023 with the release of several spectacular concert films. Two in particular rocked the box office: *Renaissance: A Film by Beyoncé* and *Taylor Swift: The Eras Tour*. Both artists struck massive deals directly with distributor AMC Entertainment to screen their movies in theaters, with huge success. Other concert films released in 2023 included *BTS: Yet to Come* and *Stop Making Sense*, which first came out in 1984, showcasing a 1983 performance by the rock band Talking Heads.

LONGEST-RUNNING SCRIPTED TV SHOW IN THE UNITED STATES
THE SIMPSONS

The Simpsons entered its thirty-fifth season in 2023, continuing to break its own record as the longest-running American sitcom, cartoon, and scripted prime-time television show in history. The animated comedy, which first aired in December 1989, centers on the antics and everyday lives of the Simpson family. Famous guest stars who have made appearances in the show include Stephen Hawking, Kelsey Grammer, and Ed Sheeran (as Lisa's new crush). Fox has renewed the show for a thirty-sixth season, which will see it air its 800th episode.

CHILDREN'S/FAMILY SHOW WITH THE **MOST** EMMYS

HEARTSTOPPER

Taking five total awards at the 2022 Children's & Family Emmys, Netflix's *Heartstopper* is the winningest show in the ceremony's history so far. Based on a hugely successful graphic novel series of the same name, *Heartstopper* won awards for Outstanding Young Teen Series and for Outstanding Casting, while its creator, Alice Oseman, won for Outstanding Writing. The show's stars also did well: Kit Connor won Outstanding Lead Performance for his role as romantic lead Nick Nelson, while Olivia Colman won the award for Outstanding Guest Actor for playing his mom.

JEOPARDY!

Jeopardy!, which entered its fortieth season in September 2023, remains the most popular game show on television with about 20 million viewers per week. The show's continuing success following the loss of its late host, Alex Trebek, led the network to renew *Jeopardy!* for another five seasons into 2027–2028, alongside sister show *Wheel of Fortune*. *Jeopardy!* host Ken Jennings kicked off the season hosting a Second Chance Tournament, in which players from season thirty-eight were welcomed back to the show's stage. In 2023, the Writers Guild of America went on strike, which meant *Jeopardy!* had to use questions drafted during previous seasons. December 2023 saw *Jeopardy!* air its 9,000th episode.

Nintendo's most famous game hit the big screen in April 2023, with *The Super Mario Bros. Movie*, an animated adventure with Chris Pratt voicing the titular Mario. Taking $574.9 million in the US, it was the highest-grossing kids' film of the year. It also passed the billion-dollar mark worldwide, becoming the most successful movie based on a video game ever made. The movie is an origin story for the game's beloved characters Mario and Luigi, who are transported from their real lives as Italian American plumbers in New York to become heroes in the fantastic Mushroom Kingdom, which is under threat from the evil Bowser.

NO. 1 KIDS' MOVIE
AT THE US BOX OFFICE
THE SUPER MARIO BROS. MOVIE

SUPER BOWL LVII

MOST-WATCHED TELEVISION BROADCAST OF 2023

Not surprisingly, 2023 saw the Super Bowl yet again take the top spot as the year's most-watched TV broadcast. Super Bowl LVII attracted nearly 115 million viewers for the Kansas City Chiefs' 38–35 victory over the Philadelphia Eagles, beating 2022's total of 112.3 million. Continuing an upward trend, football accounted for 93 of the top 100 most-watched television shows in 2023, beating the 2022 figure of 82. The highest-ranking non-football broadcast was the Oscars ceremony, which came in 15th place with 19.4 million viewers.

ONE PIECE

MOST POPULAR SHOW IN THE MOST COUNTRIES

The live-action adaptation of *One Piece* set a Netflix record when it became the streaming service's highest-ranked show in a whopping eighty-four countries upon its release weekend. Previous Netflix successes *Stranger Things* and *Wednesday* had reached no. 1 in eighty-three countries. *One Piece* is based on a 1997 manga—a Japanese comic style—about a group called the Straw Hat Pirates searching for some legendary booty. In its opening weekend, from August 31 to September 3, *One Piece* was streamed 18.5 million times. The show's popularity no doubt came as a relief for Netflix, who reportedly spent $17 million on each of its eight episodes.

MOST SUCCESSFUL MOVIE FRANCHISE
MARVEL CINEMATIC UNIVERSE

The Marvel Cinematic Universe franchise has grossed more than $27.9 billion worldwide! This impressive total includes ticket sales from the huge hits of 2018, *Black Panther* and *Avengers: Infinity War. Black Panther* grossed $1.34 billion worldwide within three months of its release, but then *Avengers: Infinity War* hit the screens, taking in $1.82 billion worldwide in its first month. With *Avengers: Endgame* earning even greater revenues in 2019, as well as the successful launch of Marvel's Phase Four in 2021 and continued excitement for the franchise, the Marvel Cinematic Universe looks set to hold this record for the foreseeable future.

MOST SUCCESSFUL MOVIE FRANCHISES
TOTAL WORLDWIDE GROSS, IN BILLIONS OF US DOLLARS (AS OF JANUARY 2023)

Franchise	$ billions
Marvel Cinematic Universe	29.8
Star Wars	10.3
Harry Potter	9.6
Spider-Man	9
James Bond	7.9

$ billions

0   5   10   15   20   25   30

MICHELLE YEOH

FIRST ASIAN WOMAN TO WIN BEST ACTRESS AT THE OSCARS

Malaysian-born Michelle Yeoh made Oscar history at the 2023 Academy Awards, becoming the first Asian woman to win the award for Best Actress. Yeoh won the Oscar for her role in *Everything Everywhere All at Once*, in which she plays a middle-aged Chinese American laundromat owner who gains superpowers and experiences different lives in multiple parallel universes. The adventure-packed film is at once funny and charming, with Yeoh performing most of her own stunts. At the awards, Yeoh accepted her Oscar with an emotional speech that included the words: "For all the little boys and girls who look like me watching tonight, this is proof that dreams do come true."

YOUNGEST ACTRESS
NOMINATED FOR AN OSCAR

QUVENZHANÉ
WALLIS

At nine years old, Quvenzhané Wallis became the youngest-ever Academy Award nominee for Best Actress. She received the nomination in 2013 for her role as Hushpuppy in *Beasts of the Southern Wild*. Although Wallis did not win the Oscar, she went on to gain forty-one more nominations and win twenty-four acting honors at various industry awards shows. In 2015, she received a Golden Globe Best Actress nomination for her role in *Annie*. Wallis was five years old when she auditioned for Hushpuppy, and she won the part over four thousand other candidates.

Justin Henry was just eight years old when he received a Best Supporting Actor nomination in 1980 for a role he played at age seven. His neighbor, a casting director, suggested that Henry try out for the part. Although the young actor lost out on the Oscar, *Kramer vs. Kramer* won several, including Best Actor for Dustin Hoffman, Best Actress in a Supporting Role for Meryl Streep, and Best Picture. Justin Henry appeared in a few other films before leaving acting to finish his education. He returned to acting in the 1990s.

YOUNGEST ACTOR NOMINATED FOR AN OSCAR

JUSTIN HENRY

TOP-EARNING KID YOUTUBER
RYAN KAJI

Ryan Kaji, the star of *Ryan's World*, made $30 million in 2022 as the highest-earning kid on YouTube at eleven years old. *Ryan's World* has attracted more than 36 million subscribers, with the number set to keep on growing. In 2017, Kaji became the youngest-ever person on a *Forbes* top-earners list when his channel made $11 million. At the time, he was just six years old! His content has changed since then, from reviewing toys to posting educational videos about his interests in the sciences, arts and crafts, and music. Videos on *Ryan's World* also feature his parents and his younger sisters, twins Emma and Kate.

T-SERIES

MOST POPULAR YOUTUBE CHANNEL

Music can change the world—or so says T-Series, the company that knocked MrBeast and Cocomelon off the top spots to become the most-subscribed channel on YouTube. The channel belongs to India's biggest music label and had an amazing 258 million subscribers at the end of 2023. The channel's popularity is boosted by its ties to Bollywood, posting movie soundtracks and trailers, as well as Indi-pop music. It's estimated that up to 40 percent of the channel's viewers come from outside India, with many of these viewers based in the US.

HIGHEST-PAID ACTRESS
MARGOT ROBBIE

In March 2024, *Forbes* named Australian actress Margot Robbie the world's highest-paid actress of 2023, with earnings of $59 million. This impressive income is mostly attributed to her role as "stereotypical Barbie" in that year's top-grossing movie, *Barbie*, directed by Greta Gerwig, for which Robbie is also credited as a producer. Since arriving in the US in the 2010s, Robbie has starred in movies by leading directors Martin Scorsese, Quentin Tarantino, and Wes Anderson, in roles alongside actors Leonardo DiCaprio, Brad Pitt, Christian Bale, and—in *Barbie*—Ryan Gosling. At thirty-three years of age, she is the youngest person on the highest-paid list and beat out Jennifer Aniston, the only other actress in the top ten, with earnings of $42 million.

The highest-paid actor of 2023, according to *Forbes*, was Adam Sandler. His $73 million is largely attributed to revenue from a four-picture deal he made in 2014 with the streaming service Netflix that was extended in 2020 to four more movies. The eight movies continue to draw huge viewership figures. The site also streams movies made by Sandler's own film production company, Happy Madison Productions, among them the 2023 hits *Murder Mystery 2*, *You Are So Not Invited to My Bat Mitzvah*, and *Leo*, an animated musical in which Sandler gives voice to a seventy-four-year-old lizard. A portion of the star's income also came from the forty-four stand-up comedy shows he gave that year.

HIGHEST-PAID ACTOR
ADAM SANDLER

TOP-GROSSING US MOVIE *BARBIE*

California-born director Greta Gerwig's *Barbie* took the world by storm in July 2023. The film smashed box-office records to become the highest-grossing film in the US by a female director—ever—earning $636 million! It was also the highest-grossing film in the 100-year history of Warner Bros. Studios. Margot Robbie's turn as Barbie also sparked a rush of collaborations, merchandising, and fashion trends—in part thanks to the film's reported astronomical $150 million marketing budget. *Barbie*'s release coincided with the opening of gritty historical drama *Oppenheimer*, with many moviegoers catching what was christened "Barbenheimer" as a double feature.

TOP-GROSSING MOVIES IN THE US
IN MILLIONS OF US DOLLARS

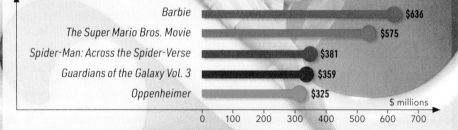

Movie	$ millions
Barbie	$636
The Super Mario Bros. Movie	$575
Spider-Man: Across the Spider-Verse	$381
Guardians of the Galaxy Vol. 3	$359
Oppenheimer	$325

$ millions
0 100 200 300 400 500 600 700

DESPICABLE ME

TOP-GROSSING
ANIMATED-FILM FRANCHISE

Following the 2022 release of *Minions: The Rise of Gru*, and with a global total of $4.64 billion, Despicable Me remains the world's highest-grossing animated franchise of all time. The 2015 spin-off, *Minions*, is the most profitable animated film in Universal Studios' history and was the highest-grossing film of the year, while *Despicable Me 3* and Oscar-nominated *Despicable Me 2* hit no. 2 in their respective years of release. Collectively, the four movies beat the Shrek franchise's earnings of $3.55 billion. In 2019, *Frozen II* became the biggest-selling animated movie ever with earnings of $1.45 billion worldwide.

PHANTOM OF THE OPERA

Marking the end of an impressive thirty-five years on Broadway, the cast of Andrew Lloyd Webber's *The Phantom of the Opera* made its last appearance on April 16, 2023. The show has been performed 13,981 times, making it the longest-running Broadway show ever. The story, based on a novel published in 1910 by French author Gaston Leroux, tells the tragic tale of the phantom and his love for an opera singer, Christine.

LION KING
HIGHEST-GROSSING BROADWAY MUSICAL

Since opening on November 13, 1997, *The Lion King* musical has earned more than $1.8 billion. It's Broadway's third-longest-running production and is an adaptation of the hugely popular Disney animated film. Along with hit songs from the movie such as "Circle of Life" and "Hakuna Matata," the show includes new compositions by South African composer Lebo M. and others. The Broadway show features songs in six African languages, including Swahili and Congolese. Since it opened, *The Lion King* has attracted audiences totaling over 100 million people.

MUSICAL WITH THE MOST TONY AWARD NOMINATIONS
HAMILTON

Lin-Manuel Miranda's musical biography of Founding Father Alexander Hamilton racked up sixteen Tony Award nominations to unseat the previous record holders, *The Producers* and *Billy Elliot: The Musical*, both of which had fifteen. The megahit hip-hop musical, which was inspired by historian Ron Chernow's biography of the first secretary of the treasury, portrays the Founding Fathers of the United States engaging in rap battles over issues such as the national debt and the French Revolution. *Hamilton* won eleven Tonys at the 2016 ceremony—one shy of *The Producers*, which retains the record for most Tony wins with twelve. *Hamilton*'s Broadway success paved the way for the show to open in Chicago in 2016, with a touring show and a London production following in 2017.

YOUNGEST WINNER OF A LAURENCE OLIVIER AWARD

ELEANOR WORTHINGTON-COX CLEO DEMETRIOU KERRY INGRAM SOPHIA KIELY

In 2012, four actresses shared an Olivier Award for their roles in the British production of *Matilda*. Eleanor Worthington-Cox, Cleo Demetriou, Kerry Ingram, and Sophia Kiely all won the award for Best Actress in a Musical. Of the four actresses, Worthington-Cox, age ten, was the youngest by a few weeks. Each actress portraying *Matilda* performs two shows a week. In the United States, the four *Matilda* actresses won a special Tony Honors for Excellence in the Theatre in 2013. *Matilda*, inspired by the book by Roald Dahl, won a record seven Olivier Awards in 2012.

THE WORLD'S LARGEST CRUISE SHIP

Royal Caribbean International's *Icon of the Seas* is the largest cruise ship the world has ever seen. It began its maiden voyage—a week of island-hopping in the Caribbean—at the end of January 2024. Almost 1,200 feet long, the vessel boasts twenty decks, seven swimming pools, record-breaking slides, and cabin space for up to 7,600 passengers. An average trip on the *Icon*, which promises "everything you've ever loved about every vacation," costs around $2,000 per person.

WORLD'S MOST POWERFUL ROCKET FAILS

The SpaceX Starship took to the skies in April 2023 for its first test flight but lasted only about four minutes before exploding. The world's most powerful rocket ship had two parts—the second-stage Starship spacecraft and the first-stage Super Heavy booster. After the two parts failed to separate, they were seen tumbling through the skies before breaking apart. Still, SpaceX officials celebrated the rocket making it off the ground at all, having launched and climbed up to 25 miles into the air from Starbase in Boca Chica, Texas. A second, similarly ill-fated test flight was made in November 2023.

DEEP-SEA SUBMERSIBLE IMPLODES

In June 2023, contact was lost with a deep-sea submersible visiting the wreck of the HMS *Titanic*. The sub, *Titan*, a creation of OceanGate Expeditions, held five men, including the company's founder as pilot. It lost contact an hour and forty-five minutes into the two-hour descent. Rescue efforts attempted to locate the sub. However, the discovery of a debris field confirmed that the craft had suffered a "catastrophic implosion," killing all aboard instantly.

SUSTAINABLE FLIGHT SUCCESS

Virgin Atlantic won a victory for the future of green energy in November 2023 when it sent a plane across the Atlantic Ocean, from London to New York City, with an interesting fuel source: fat and sugar! This sustainable aviation fuel (SAF) is a blend of waste fats and plant sugars, so it is not only a source of lower carbon emissions but also a potential solution for waste reduction. Virgin Atlantic's Flight100 marked the first time ever a transatlantic commercial airline flight used 100 percent SAF.

LONGEST TIME IN SPACE

A new record for the US astronaut with the longest single spaceflight goes to Dr. Frank Rubio, whose time up there lasted an amazing 371 days. Rubio, a physician and West Point graduate who served in the US Army as a helicopter pilot, arrived at the International Space Station on September 21, 2022, and documented some of his time there on his YouTube series, *A Year of Science in Space*, which featured experiments the team on the space station were conducting alongside researchers back on Earth.

WORLD'S FIRST
MONSTER
SCHOOL BUS

Bad to the Bone was the first monster school bus in the world. This revamped 1956 yellow bus is 13 feet tall, thanks to massive tires with 25-inch rims. The oversize bus weighs 19,000 pounds and is a favorite ride at charity events in California. But don't expect to get anywhere in a hurry—this "Kool Bus" is not built for speed and goes a maximum of just 7 miles per hour.

MOST EXPENSIVE MODERN STREET-LEGAL CARS
IN MILLIONS OF US DOLLARS

Car	Price ($ million)
Rolls-Royce Droptail	$30
Rolls-Royce Boat Tail	$27.8
Bugatti La Voiture Noire	$18.7
Pagani Zonda HP Barchetta	$17
SP Automotive Chaos	$14.4

$ million

5   10   15   20   25   30

In 2023, Rolls-Royce unveiled its new Droptail model, a luxury two-seat roadster with a price of more than $30 million. Its twin-turbocharged 6.75-liter V-12 engine delivers 563 horsepower—which is a *lot* of power, but nowhere near what some modern supercars offer. What makes this Rolls-Royce stand out is its elegant styling, which combines old-world craftsmanship with modern technology. More than 1,600 pieces of black sycamore wood veneer were painstakingly assembled by a craftsperson into an abstract artwork that covers portions of the vehicle's interior, while the car's removable hardtop is made from carbon fiber and electrochromic glass. The first of four customized Droptails, the 2023 version is named La Rose Noire for the Black Baccara rose that provided inspiration for the car's color and design.

MOST EXPENSIVE CAR
ROLLS-ROYCE DROPTAIL

FIRST COUNTRY TO REACH THE LUNAR SOUTH POLE INDIA

On August 23, 2023, the Indian Space Research Organization's uncrewed moon lander, *Vikram*, touched down less than 400 miles from the lunar south pole, becoming the first spacecraft to reach and explore that polar region. Scientists have discovered that this part of the moon contains frozen water—and that locating lunar water may make it possible to establish habitable bases on the moon and even create rocket fuel there. Just days before *Vikram* arrived, an uncrewed Russian lunar lander designed to explore this same area crashed into the moon's surface. With the success of this Chandrayaan-3 mission, India became only the fourth country to land on the moon, joining the United States, the former Soviet Union, and China.

QTVAN

WORLD'S SMALLEST TRAILER

The tiny QTvan is just over 7 feet long, 2.5 feet wide, and 5 feet tall. Inside, however, it has a full-size single bed, a kettle for boiling water, and a 19-inch TV. The Environmental Transport Association (ETA) in Britain sponsored the invention of the minitrailer, which was designed to be pulled by a mobility scooter. The ETA recommends the QTvan for short trips only, since mobility scooters have a top speed of 6 miles per hour, at best.

FASTEST LAND VEHICLE
THRUST SSC

The world's fastest car is the Thrust SSC, which reached a speed of 763 miles per hour on October 15, 1997, in the Black Rock Desert of Nevada. SSC stands for supersonic (faster than the speed of sound) car. The Thrust SSC's amazing speed comes from two jet engines with 110,000 brake horsepower. That's as much as 145 Formula 1 race cars. The British-made car uses about 5 gallons of jet fuel in one second and takes just five seconds to reach its top speed. At that speed, the Thrust SSC could travel from New York City to San Francisco in less than four hours. Another British manufacturer is currently developing a new supersonic car, the Bloodhound, with a projected speed of 1,000 miles per hour. If it reaches that, it will set a new world record.

FASTEST PASSENGER TRAINS
(BY MAXIMUM OPERATING SPEED)

China Shanghai Maglev
268 mph

China CR Harmony
218 mph

China CR Fuxing
218 mph

Germany ICE3
205 mph

France TGV
199 mph

Operating speed

0   50   100   150   200   250   300

The Shanghai Maglev, which runs between Shanghai Pudong International Airport and the outskirts of Shanghai, is currently the fastest passenger train in the world. The service reaches top speeds of 268 miles per hour, covering the 19-mile distance in seven minutes and twenty seconds. Maglev is short for magnetic levitation, as the train moves by floating on magnets rather than with wheels on a track. Other high-speed trains, such as Japan's SCMaglev, may have reached higher speeds in testing (375 miles per hour) but are capped at 200 miles per hour when carrying passengers.

FASTEST PASSENGER TRAIN
SHANGHAI MAGLEV

FASTEST UNPILOTED PLANE X-43A

In November 2004, NASA launched its experimental X-43A plane for a test flight over the Pacific Ocean. The X-43A plane reached Mach 9.6, which is more than nine times the speed of sound and nearly 7,000 miles per hour. A B-52 aircraft carried the X-43A and a Pegasus rocket booster into the air, releasing them at 40,000 feet. At that point, the booster—essentially a fuel-packed engine—ignited, blasting the unpiloted X-43A higher and faster, before separating from the plane. The plane continued to fly for several minutes at 110,000 feet, before crashing (intentionally) into the ocean.

The Parker Solar Probe set a new record for the fastest known human-made object on September 27, 2023, when it reached 394,736 miles per hour. Jointly operated by NASA and Johns Hopkins University, and equipped with a wide range of scientific equipment, the Parker Solar Probe is on a seven-year mission to study the Sun's atmosphere. Withstanding extreme heat and radiation, it sends data and images back to Earth, revolutionizing our understanding of the star at the heart of our solar system. That same day, the probe shattered a second record by reaching a distance of just 4.51 million miles from the solar surface—the closest a spacecraft has ever been to the Sun and less than one-twentieth of the distance between the Sun and Earth.

PARKER
SOLAR PROBE
FASTEST HUMAN-MADE OBJECT

LIFTOFF

1
2
3
4
5
6
7
8

10

APOLLO 10

NASA's Apollo 10 spacecraft reached its top speed on its descent to Earth, hurtling through the atmosphere at 24,816 miles per hour and splashing down on May 26, 1969. The spacecraft's crew had traveled faster than anyone on Earth. The mission was a dress rehearsal for the first moon landing by Apollo 11, two months later. The Apollo 10 spacecraft consisted of a Command and Service Module, called Charlie Brown, and a Lunar Module, called Snoopy. Today, Charlie Brown is on display at the Science Museum in London, England.

APOLLO 10 FLIGHT STATS

05/18/1969 Launch date

12:49 P.M. EDT Launch

05/21/1969 Date entered Lunar Orbit

192:03:23 Duration of mission: 192 hours, 3 minutes, 23 seconds

05/26/1969 Return date

12:52 P.M. EDT Splashdown

LIFTOFF

The Apollo 10 spacecraft was launched from Florida's Cape Canaveral, known as Cape Kennedy at the time. It was the fourth crewed Apollo launch in seven months.

FASTEST ROLLER COASTER
FORMULA ROSSA

Thrill seekers hurtle along the Formula Rossa track at 149.1 miles per hour. The high-speed roller coaster is part of Ferrari World in Abu Dhabi, United Arab Emirates. Ferrari World also features the world's largest indoor theme park, at 1.5 million square feet. The Formula Rossa roller-coaster seats are red Ferrari-shaped cars that travel from 0 to 62 miles per hour in just two seconds—as fast as a race car. The ride's g-force is so extreme that passengers must wear goggles to protect their eyes. g-force acts on a body due to acceleration and gravity. People can withstand 6 to 8 g's for short periods. The Formula Rossa g-force is 4.8 g's during acceleration and 1.7 g's at maximum speed.

FORMULA ROSSA WORLD RECORDS

149.1 MPH Speed

1.7 g's G-force

4.8 g's Acceleration

Rising 86 feet above Hurricane Harbor Chicago amusement park, Tsunami Surge is the tallest water coaster in the world. Psychedelic visual effects light the way as thrill seekers are blasted through 950 feet of slides, tunnels, and hairpin bends at top speeds of 28 miles per hour. This attraction—the twenty-fifth to debut at the Six Flags park—uses the latest technology in jet propulsion to power its passengers all the way up the steepest slopes . . . and down again.

TALLEST WATER COASTER
TSUNAMI SURGE

super structures trending

FREE LIGHTHOUSE, ANYONE? Each May, the General Services Administration (GSA) transfers ownership of American lighthouses to organizations willing to take over the preservation of these important—but navigationally redundant—structures and make them publicly accessible. In 2023, six free lighthouses, plus four sold at auction, marked a record number offered by the GSA since the passing of the National Historic Lighthouse Preservation Act in 2000.

ARTIST'S LEGO MASTERPIECE Chinese artist Ai Weiwei used 650,000 LEGO bricks to build *Water Lilies #1*, unveiled at London's Design Museum in March 2023. The 50-foot-long artwork is a take on paintings by 19th-century artist Claude Monet. The work also features what the museum describes as a "dark portal" representing the door to the underground dugout Ai and his father lived in during exile in the 1960s.

GREAT WALL DAMAGED The Great Wall of China took a hit in 2023 when two construction workers decided to widen an existing gap to shorten their journey. The two workers used an excavator to create a path through the wall; it was discovered and reported to police. The workers were apprehended nearby and were charged with damaging a cultural relic.

WORLD CAPITAL OF ARCHITECTURE UNESCO and the International Union of Architects (UIA) named the Danish capital city of Copenhagen as the World Capital of Architecture in 2023. The title, first designated in 2020, is awarded every three years by UNESCO-UIA, and was previously held by Rio de Janeiro, Brazil. A primary goal is for the city to become a global forum for discussions on the future of architecture and urban planning.

PARIS SKYSCRAPER BAN In 2023, the French capital, Paris, banned the construction of skyscrapers over twelve stories, or 121 feet, following the start of work on the controversial Triangle Tower in 2022. Once completed, the triangular skyscraper will be the city's third tallest building at 590 feet, but opponents have criticized its "catastrophic" carbon footprint. The ban is part of the mayor's Local Bioclimatic Urban Plan, which aims to reduce carbon emissions in the city.

HONG KONG

CITY WITH THE MOST SKYSCRAPERS

NUMBER OF SKYSCRAPERS AT 500 FEET OR HIGHER

Buildings

600	552
	390
300	316
	258
0	

Hong Kong, China
Shenzhen, China
New York City, US
Dubai, UAE

Hong Kong, China, has 552 buildings that reach 500 feet or higher, six of which are actually 1,000 feet or higher. The tallest three are the International Commerce Centre (ICC) at 1,588 feet; Two International Finance Centre at 1,352 feet; and Central Plaza at 1,227 feet. Hong Kong's stunning skyline towers above Victoria Harbour. Most of its tallest buildings are on Hong Kong Island, although the other side of the harbor, Kowloon, is growing. Every night a light, laser, and sound show called "A Symphony of Lights" illuminates the sky against a backdrop of about forty of Hong Kong's skyscrapers.

LARGEST SPORTS STADIUMS
BY CAPACITY

Rungrado 1st of May Stadium, North Korea — 150,000

Narendra Modi Stadium, Ahmedabad, India — 132,000

Michigan Stadium, Michigan, US — 107,601

Beaver Stadium, Pennsylvania, US — 106,572

Ohio Stadium, Ohio, US — 102,780

capacity

0   40,000   80,000   120,000   160,000

It took over two years to build Rungrado 1st of May Stadium, a huge sports venue that has a capacity for up to 150,000 people. The 197-foot-tall stadium opened in 1989 on Rungra Island in North Korea's capital, Pyongyang. The stadium hosts international soccer matches on its natural grass pitch and has other facilities such as an indoor swimming pool, training halls, and a 1,312-foot rubberized running track. A newcomer to the list, the second-largest venue, India's Narendra Modi Stadium, was inaugurated in 2020.

WORLD'S LARGEST SPORTS STADIUM

RUNGRADO
1ST OF MAY STADIUM

WORLD'S MOST EXPENSIVE HOTEL
LOVER'S DEEP

The spectacular *Lover's Deep*, a luxury submarine that spends the night touring the underwater world of St. Lucia in the Caribbean Sea, is currently the world's most expensive hotel. Attended by their own personal butler, guests sleep in spacious quarters full of extravagant furnishings, including a minibar area. As they sit back and relax, huge wraparound windows provide an ever-changing view of the colorful marine life outside. And the cost? Packages vary, but guests booking into the submarine can expect to spend a minimum of $150,000 for just one night.

TOWN WHERE MORE THAN HALF THE RESIDENTS LIVE UNDERGROUND
COOBER PEDY
AUSTRALIA

Some 60 percent of this Australian mining town's approximately 2,500 residents live in cave-like homes that are dug into the ground, not constructed above it. The region's scalding summer temperatures are the reason for these unusual homes. Surface temperatures in Coober Pedy often climb above 120°F, but belowground remain comfortably in the mid-70s year-round. Called the opal capital of the world—the majority of Earth's opals come from this area—Coober Pedy also has underground churches, museums, hotel rooms, and campsites. The region's sandstone is structurally sound but also relatively easy to carve away— when Coober Pedy's subterranean homeowners want extra living space, they simply dig out new rooms for themselves, no contractors or lumber required.

GOING
UP

BURJ KHALIFA

LAID END TO END, THE STEEL USED HERE WOULD STRETCH ONE QUARTER OF THE WAY AROUND THE WORLD!

Holding the record for the world's tallest building since January 2010, the Burj Khalifa is 2,716.5 feet tall. It not only qualifies as the world's tallest building, but also the tallest human-made structure, the tallest freestanding structure, having the largest number of stories, and the highest aluminum and glass facades (which incidentally cover the same area as twenty-five football fields). The tower took six years to build, with 12,000 men on-site day after day, completing twenty-two million hours of work. Dubbed a "vertical city," the tower holds around 10,000 people at any given time.

DUBAI'S BURJ KHALIFA WORLD RECORDS:

1,654 **FEET** Tallest elevator inside a building

163 Number of floors

1,448 **FEET** Highest restaurant from ground level

TOUGH CLIMB

No fewer than 2,909 steps lead up to floor 160 of the Burj Khalifa. Anyone wishing to go higher has to do so climbing ladders.

WORLD'S LARGEST
FREESTANDING BUILDING
NEW CENTURY
GLOBAL CENTER

The New Century Global Center in Chengdu, southwestern China, is a huge 18.9 million square feet. That's nearly three times the size of the Pentagon in Arlington, Virginia. Completed in 2013, the structure is 328 feet tall, 1,640 feet long, and 1,312 feet deep. The building houses a 4.3-million-square-foot shopping mall, two hotels, an Olympic-size ice rink, a fourteen-screen IMAX cinema complex, and offices. It even has its own Paradise Island, a beach resort complete with artificial sun.

LARGEST SWIMMING POOLS
SIZE IN ACRES

Pool	Acres
Citystars Sharm El Sheikh, Egypt	29.7
San Alfonso del Mar, Algarrobo, Chile	19.8
MahaSamutr, Hua Hin, Thailand	17.8
Ostrava Poruba, Czech Republic	10.2
Diamante Cabo San Lucas, Mexico	10.0

acres: 0 5 10 15 20 25 30

WORLD'S LARGEST SWIMMING POOL
CITYSTARS POOL

Citystars Sharm El Sheikh lagoon in Egypt stretches over 29.7 acres. It was created by Crystal Lagoons, the same company that built the former record holder at San Alfonso del Mar in Chile. The lagoon at Sharm El Sheikh cost $5.5 million to create and is designed to be sustainable, using salt water from local underground aquifers. The creators purify this water not just for recreation, but also to provide clean, fresh water to the surrounding community.

WORLD'S LONGEST BRIDGE
DANYANG-KUNSHAN
GRAND BRIDGE

Crossing the floodplain of China's Yangtze River, a terrain of hills, lakes, flatlands, and rice paddies, the 102-mile-long Danyang-Kunshan Grand Bridge is the longest bridge in the world. It is a viaduct, which means it is built using many short spans rather than one long one. The spans are raised 328 feet above the ground, on average, and are supported on 2,000 pillars. It's a design that helps the high-speed rail bridge to cross the ever-changing landscape between the Chinese cities of Shanghai and Nanjing. Costing $8.5 billion to construct, the bridge took four years to build using a task force of 10,000 laborers.

The world's most sustainable city is Oslo, the capital city of Norway, according to the most recent update of the Arcadis Sustainable Cities Index. Extremely low air pollution and huge amounts of green space help Oslo land at the top of this list—47 percent of this city is covered in plant life. Oslo also has made a strong commitment to renewable energy—hydropower provides more than half of this city's total electricity, and electric cars are so common here that Oslo has been labeled the EV Capital of the World. This city of more than one million people is on track to reach its goal of nearly zero emissions by 2030. Ranking right behind Oslo in the sustainable cities index are Stockholm, Tokyo, Copenhagen, Berlin, London, and Seattle.

OSLO

WORLD'S MOST SUSTAINABLE CITY

WORLD'S LARGEST LIVING WALL
KHALIFA AVENUE
QATAR

Completed in 2020, the Khalifa Avenue living wall in Doha, Qatar, features more than 75,000 square feet of lush plant life situated on nearly vertical surfaces along the sides of an elevated roadway. That's a green space significantly larger than a football field—but unlike a football field, this greenery is growing on a wall. Qatari company Nakheel Landscapes installed the wall using the ANS Living Wall System pioneered by British company ANS Global. Living walls—also known as green walls or vertical gardens—not only look beautiful, but they also improve air quality in urban areas. One challenge for Khalifa Avenue's builders is that local temperatures regularly climb above 120°F in the summer, which is much too hot for many plants.

Launched on December 25, 2021, the James Webb Space Telescope is the largest space telescope ever. While its forerunner, the Hubble Space Telescope, is roughly the size of a school bus, the Webb is more like the size of a tennis court. It is so big that it had to be folded up inside a rocket for launching. It was not until January 8, 2022, that the telescope's mirror fully unfolded for use, and it has now reached its destination some 930,000 miles away from Earth. The Webb is about one hundred times more powerful than its predecessor. Since July 12, 2022, NASA has released many spectacular color images captured by the telescope, revealing some of the earliest stars and galaxies in the universe.

LARGEST-EVER SPACE TELESCOPE
JAMES WEBB
SPACE TELESCOPE

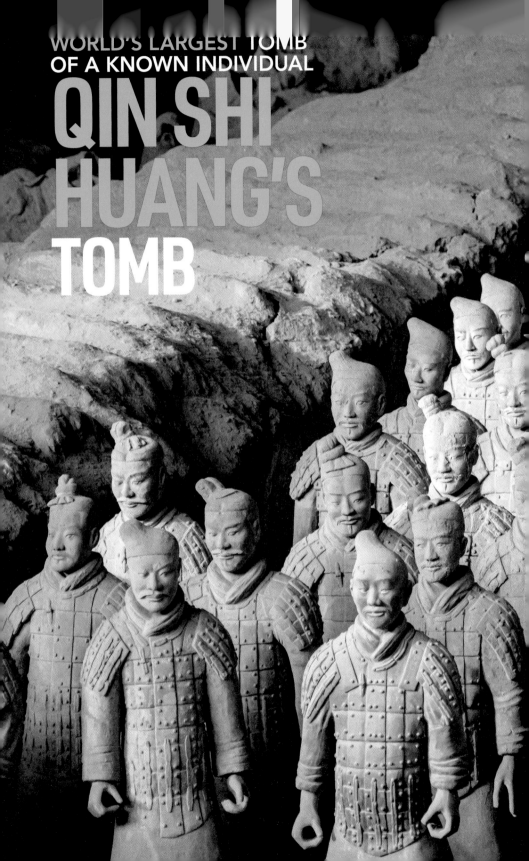

QIN SHI HUANG'S TOMB

Emperor Qin Shi Huang ruled China in the third century BCE. In 1974, people digging a well in the fields northeast of Xi'an, in the Shaanxi province, accidentally discovered the ancient tomb. Further investigation revealed a burial complex of over 20 square miles. A large pit contained 6,000 life-size terra-cotta warrior figures, each one different from the next and dressed according to rank. A second pit and third contained 2,000 more figures; clay horses; about 40,000 bronze weapons; and other artifacts. Historians think that 700,000 people worked for about thirty-six years to create this incredible mausoleum. The emperor's tomb remains sealed to preserve its contents and to protect workers from possible hazards, such as chemical poisoning from mercury in the surrounding soil.

QIN SHI HUANG'S TOMB

1974 Year of discovery

36 Number of years to create

8,000 Total number of figures found

221–210 BCE Duration of Qin Shi Huang's reign

FIRST EMPEROR OF CHINA

Emperor Qin Shi Huang was the first emperor of a unified China. Before his rule, the territory had been a collection of independent states. He was just forty-nine years old when he died.

WORLD'S LARGEST ANCIENT CASTLE
PRAGUE CASTLE

According to Guinness World Records, Prague Castle, founded in the late-ninth century CE, is the largest ancient castle complex in the world. Covering an area of 750,000 square feet, the castle grounds span enough land for seven football fields, with buildings in various architectural styles that have been added and renovated during past centuries. They include the famous St. Vitus Cathedral. Formerly the home of kings and emperors, the castle is now occupied by the president of the Czech Republic and his family and is also open to tourists.

The record for the world's tallest sandcastle, standing at an impressive 69 feet, 5 inches tall, was set on July 2, 2021, in the Blokhus Sculpture Park, Denmark. Built in a bid to raise morale in the seaside town of Blokhus in the wake of the COVID-19 pandemic, the sandcastle is more than 10 feet taller than the previous record holder. It was created by Wilfred Stijger and a team of thirty sand sculptors and includes local sights and coastal sports among its features. Right at the top is a sculpture of the virus that causes COVID-19 wearing a crown.

WORLD'S TALLEST SANDCASTLE
BLOKHUS SCULPTURE PARK DENMARK

WORLD'S LONGEST LEGO® SHIP
WORLD DREAM

In 2017, 1,000 cruise passengers and volunteers came together to help build a replica of the *World Dream* cruise ship, a vessel owned by China's Dream Cruises Management Ltd. Boasting more than 2.5 million LEGO blocks, this spectacle is the longest LEGO ship ever built. It's a complete scaled-down replica of the *World Dream* cruise ship, with all eighteen of its decks, and measures 27 feet, 8.5 inches in length. Upon completion, it was placed in Hong Kong's Kai Tak Cruise Terminal for all to see.

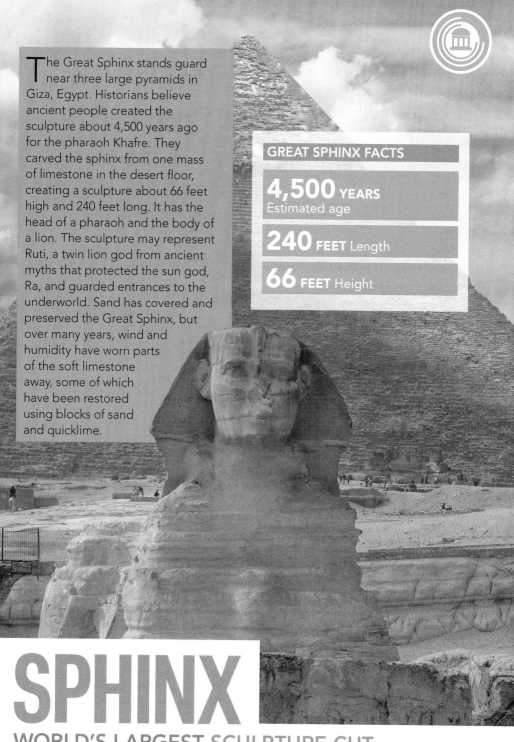

The Great Sphinx stands guard near three large pyramids in Giza, Egypt. Historians believe ancient people created the sculpture about 4,500 years ago for the pharaoh Khafre. They carved the sphinx from one mass of limestone in the desert floor, creating a sculpture about 66 feet high and 240 feet long. It has the head of a pharaoh and the body of a lion. The sculpture may represent Ruti, a twin lion god from ancient myths that protected the sun god, Ra, and guarded entrances to the underworld. Sand has covered and preserved the Great Sphinx, but over many years, wind and humidity have worn parts of the soft limestone away, some of which have been restored using blocks of sand and quicklime.

GREAT SPHINX FACTS

4,500 YEARS
Estimated age

240 FEET Length

66 FEET Height

SPHINX

WORLD'S LARGEST SCULPTURE CUT FROM A SINGLE PIECE OF STONE

ELEKTRON
AUF HÖCH

HIGH TECH trending

LONG-TIME VOICE ACTOR RETIRES Charles Martinet, the voice of Nintendo game characters Mario, Luigi, Wario, and Waluigi, has retired. The American actor began voicing the beloved Italian plumbers in the early 1990s and became famous after the release of *Super Mario 64* in 1996, which has sold about 12 million copies worldwide. Catchphrases such as "It's-a me, Mario!" and "Mamma mia!" are now iconic.

PARALYZED MAN WALKS AGAIN Thanks to state-of-the-art technology, Gert-Jan Oskam can walk again. A biking accident had left the Dutch forty-year-old without the use of his legs. But now he has implants in his brain and spinal cord and wears a headset with sensors. When he wants to move, the sensors pick up signals in his brain and send them to the spinal implant. Then the muscles get the message, and Oskam can move his legs. Today, he can walk about 330 feet at a time and can even climb stairs.

UNVEILING INDIGENOUS HISTORY

A new tool allows people to learn about the history of the place where they live. With Native Land Digital's interactive map, users can type in their location to discover which Indigenous communities lived there in the past. Links on the map lead to more information. Native Land Digital's website also includes a teacher's guide and information about Indigenous languages and land treaties. The mobile app enables users to drop a pin on the map to find out more about a given location.

THREE-DIMENSIONAL AZTEC CITY

For the first time, people can see Tenochtitlán (now the site of Mexico City) as it was before Spanish conquistadors destroyed it in 1521. Dutch video game software developer Thomas Kole spent a year and a half researching its history. The result is *A Portrait of Tenochtitlán*, a 3D reconstruction of the Aztec city as it would have looked in 1518, with close-up views of Templo Mayor (Main Temple), homes, canals, and the surrounding landscape.

POKÉMON CRACKDOWN

In 2023, several players were disqualified for using hacked Pokémon at the Pokémon World Tournament in Yokohama, Japan. Each August, the best Pokémon players in the world are invited to compete in the tournament, which has a prize pool of $500,000 across four disciplines, including the Video Game Championships (VGC). Many VGC players save time and money by using a program to breed, train, or modify their Pokémon, but it is against the rules to use these hacked characters in tournaments. This was the first time, however, that organizers enforced those rules.

CRISTIANO
RONALDO

Portuguese soccer icon Cristiano Ronaldo may once again be the year's most-followed celebrity on Instagram. In December 2023, he had 614 million followers. In 2022, Ronaldo became the first player to score at five consecutive FIFA World Cups (2006–2022). However, his hopes of becoming a World Cup champion were dashed when Portugal was beaten 1–0 by Morocco in the quarterfinals. Instead, that honor went to longtime rival Lionel Messi, whose increased popularity saw him climb to the second position on the list, with more than 494 million followers as of December 2023.

YUSAKU MAEZAWA

MOST RETWEETED TWEET EVER

Yusaku Maezawa holds the title for most retweeted tweet of all time, with a whopping 4.4 million retweets. Celebrating his company's high Christmas–New Year earnings in 2018–2019, the Japanese billionaire posted a tweet with accompanying images promising to split one hundred million yen ($937,638) among one hundred randomly chosen people. Another giveaway from Yusaku (who tweets as @yousuck2020) also made the list as the second-most retweeted tweet. The prospect of free money definitely helped motivate people to make this one go viral!

MONOPOLY GO

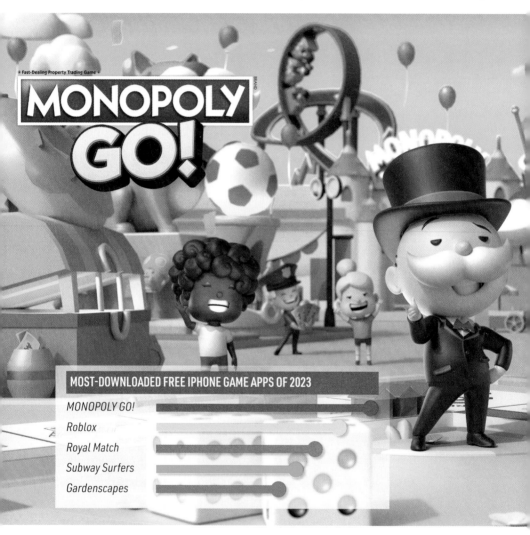

MOST-DOWNLOADED FREE IPHONE GAME APPS OF 2023

MONOPOLY GO!

Roblox

Royal Match

Subway Surfers

Gardenscapes

MONOPOLY GO!, a reimagined version of the classic board game *Monopoly*, was downloaded more than any other free iPhone game in the US in 2023, according to Apple. *Subway Surfers*, the most downloaded game of 2022, landed at number four on Apple's list. Meanwhile, a more traditional digital version of *Monopoly* landed at number five on Apple's list of 2023's top paid iPhone games— *Minecraft* took the top spot there. Overall, 2023 was a very impressive year for *Monopoly*, a game that dates back to the 1930s.

The addictive "Baby Shark Dance" video by South Korean brand Pinkfong has been viewed at least 13 billion times since its upload in June 2016, making it the most-viewed YouTube video ever. The simple song and its accompanying dance moves went viral in 2018, and "Baby Shark Dance" now has its own line of merchandise, as well as an animated series on Nickelodeon. There is even a remix starring Luis Fonsi, which is ironic, given that Fonsi's "Despacito" held the no. 1 spot prior to "Baby Shark Dance."

MOST-VIEWED YOUTUBE VIDEO EVER
"BABY SHARK DANCE"

MOST POPULAR NEW EMOJI
PINK HEART

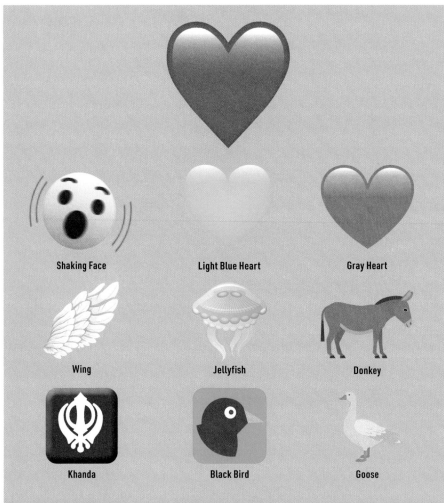

Shaking Face

Light Blue Heart

Gray Heart

Wing

Jellyfish

Donkey

Khanda

Black Bird

Goose

According to online resource Emojipedia, the most popular new emoji in 2023 was Pink Heart. The announcement was made for the site's World Emoji Awards, which it gives out annually in celebration of World Emoji Day, July 17. Runners-up in this year's awards were Shaking Face, in second, and Light Blue Heart, in third, according to data collated from Emojipedia's page views between September 13, 2022, and July 10, 2023. And, if you are wondering why July 17 was chosen for World Emoji Day, it's because this is the date shown on the Calendar emoji!

In June 2020, "Justice for George Floyd" became Change.org's most-signed petition ever, with 19 million signatures. The petition called for the four police officers involved in Floyd's death to be fired and arrested. George Floyd, a Black man, died on May 25 after white officer Derek Chauvin knelt on his neck for about nine minutes during an arrest, with three fellow officers standing by. Video footage of the event went viral, sparking antiracism protests across the globe. In April 2021, Derek Chauvin was found guilty of three charges for killing George Floyd.

MOST-SIGNED CHANGE.ORG PETITION

JUSTICE FOR GEORGE FLOYD

MOST-VIEWED TIKTOK VIDEO
ZACH KING

P roving that the world still loves watching magic, three of the five most-viewed videos on the TikTok platform come from American illusionist Zach King. The most popular TikTok video ever, with 2.3 billion views, shows King pulling off a Harry Potter–based trick in which he uses a long board and mirrored surface to create the illusion of flying on a broomstick down a California street. The only TikToks in the top five that are not by King come from makeup YouTuber James Charles, with his "Sisters Christmas Party" (2019), which has 1.8 billion views, and Bella Poarch's "M to the B" video (2020) with more than 691 million views.

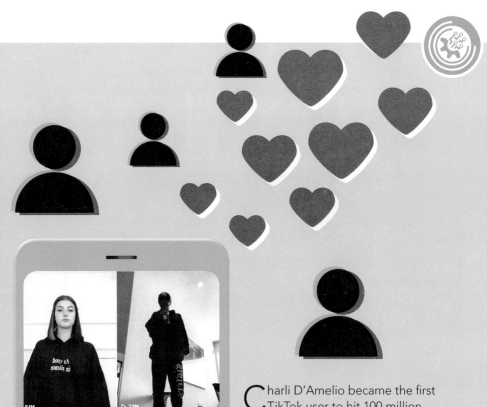

Charli D'Amelio became the first TikTok user to hit 100 million followers on the app in November 2020, when she was only sixteen years old. The social media personality, who joined the app in 2019, quickly became known for her lip-syncing and dancing challenge videos. Her one hundred million milestone came at a controversial time, with D'Amelio losing around one million followers for her behavior in a "Dinner with the D'Amelios" YouTube segment. Despite this, D'Amelio's online presence has earned her an estimated net worth of $17.5 million, including income from movie roles and brand partnerships.

FIRST ACCOUNT TO REACH **100M** ON TIKTOK

CHARLI D'AMELIO

DOUG THE PUG

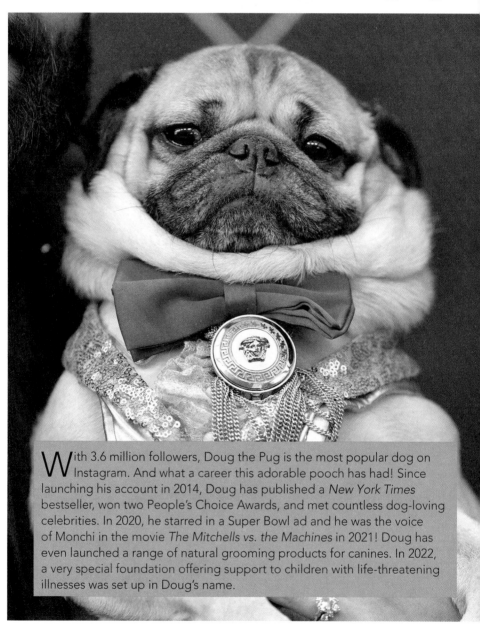

With 3.6 million followers, Doug the Pug is the most popular dog on Instagram. And what a career this adorable pooch has had! Since launching his account in 2014, Doug has published a *New York Times* bestseller, won two People's Choice Awards, and met countless dog-loving celebrities. In 2020, he starred in a Super Bowl ad and he was the voice of Monchi in the movie *The Mitchells vs. the Machines* in 2021! Doug has even launched a range of natural grooming products for canines. In 2022, a very special foundation offering support to children with life-threatening illnesses was set up in Doug's name.

In January 2020, and with a total of 4.3 million followers, Nala Cat broke the Guinness World Record for the cat with the most followers on Instagram. As of December 2023, the feline remains just as popular with 4.5 million. Adopted from a shelter at just five months old, the Siamese-tabby charms online viewers around the world with her bright blue eyes and supercute headgear.

CAT WITH THE MOST INSTAGRAM FOLLOWERS

NALA CAT

RECORD POKÉMON COLLECTION

POKÉMON
MERCHANDISE

The largest-ever collection of Pokémon merchandise made the news in 2022 after its British collector decided to put it up for auction. This impressive hoard includes more than 20,000 items acquired from around the world—including clothing, cards, plushies, and video games from the UK, US, Japan, Germany, and more. It represents more than twenty-five years of collecting, beginning when the owner was just nine years old. Some of the rarer (and stranger!) things she found include cans of Pokémon-shaped spaghetti and even Pokémon-printed toilet paper! All of these treasures were due to be auctioned in Derbyshire, UK, in October 2022, at a reserve price of £300,000. Despite the high demand for Pokémon items, this was too high a price to pay for even the most avid collector, and the lot failed to sell.

TETRIS

Tetris, developed by Russian computer scientist Alexey Pajitnov in 1984, has sold over 500 million copies worldwide—more than any other game. It has been available on almost every video game console since its creation and has seen a resurgence in sales as an app for cell phones and tablets. The iconic puzzle game was the first video game to be exported from the Soviet Union to the United States and the first to be played in outer space, and is often listed as one of the best video games of all time. In 2019, Nintendo released *Tetris 99* for Nintendo Switch—a multiplayer version of the game that sees ninety-nine players compete against one another online.

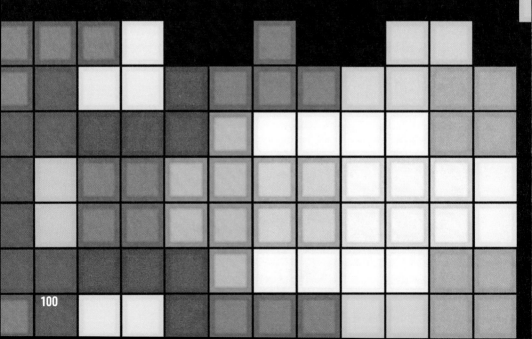

HOGWARTS LEGACY

BEST-SELLING VIDEO GAME OF 2023

With sales of more than 22 million copies worldwide, *Hogwarts Legacy*, an immersive role-playing game, was the best-selling game in the US in 2023. Released on February 10, the Warner Brothers Games title is set in the universe of the best-selling Harry Potter novels, but the action takes place more than a century before the events of the classic series. Released in November 2023, the game's biggest rival, *Call of Duty: Modern Warfare III*, made the no. 2 slot in the listings. The sports game *Madden NFL 24*, released on August 18, came in at no. 3.

BEST-SELLING
CONSOLE OF ALL TIME
PS2

PlayStation's legendary console, the PS2, is still the best-selling console of all time, with parent company Sony confirming the sale of more than 159 million units. Launched in 2000, the PS2 was particularly successful because it could play PS2 games, PS1 games, and even DVDs. In second place, with around 154 million units sold, is the Nintendo DS, released in 2004 and now discontinued, and in third place is the Nintendo Switch, with 129.5 million units sold.

Nintendo's *Mario* franchise has sold 832 million units since the first game was released in 1983. Since then, Mario, his brother Luigi, and other characters like Princess Peach and Yoshi have become household names, starring in a number of games. In the early games, like *Super Mario World*, players jump over obstacles, collect tokens, and capture flags as Mario journeys through the Mushroom Kingdom to save the princess. The franchise has since diversified to include other popular games, such as *Mario Kart*, a racing game showcasing the inhabitants and landscapes of the Mushroom Kingdom.

BEST-SELLING VIDEO GAME FRANCHISE OF ALL TIME
MARIO

According to the Guinness World Records, Minefaire 2016, a huge gathering of *Minecraft* fans, was the biggest convention ever for a single video game. Held October 15–16 at the Greater Philadelphia Expo Center in Oaks, Pennsylvania, the event attracted 12,140 people. Game developer Markus Persson created *Minecraft* in 2009 and sold it to Microsoft in 2014 for $2.5 billion. Gamers can play alone or with other players online. The game involves breaking and placing blocks to build whatever gamers can imagine—from simple constructions to huge virtual worlds. Attendance was not the only element of Minefaire to gain world-record status. On October 15, the largest-ever *Minecraft* architecture lesson attracted 342 attendees, and American gamer Lestat Wade broke the record for building the tallest staircase in *Minecraft* in one minute.

MINEFAIRE 2016

MINEFAIRE STATS

12,140 Number of people attending Minefaire

150,000 Total area, in square feet, of *Minecraft*-centered attractions

3 Number of Guinness World Records broken at the fair

MR**BEAST**

Jimmy Donaldson, better known as MrBeast, is famed for his outlandish and generous YouTube giveaways—$10,000 to sit in a bathtub of snakes, anyone?—so it should surprise nobody that he's also raking in the cash. In 2023, his $82 million in earnings made him the highest-grossing YouTuber of all time. He also made a bold foray into the food industry, creating the "MrBeast Burger" virtual restaurant brand, which partners with existing restaurants around the United States to make and deliver his menu.

VERSIUS
WORLD'S SMALLEST SURGICAL ROBOT

British robot specialist Cambridge Medical Robotics developed the world's smallest surgical robot in 2017. Operated by a surgeon using a console guide with a 3D screen, the robot is able to carry out keyhole surgery. The scientists modeled the robot, called Versius, on the human arm, giving it similar wrist joints to allow maximum flexibility. Keyhole surgery involves making very small cuts on the surface of a person's body, through which a surgeon can then operate. The recovery time of the patient is usually quicker when operated on in this way.

BIGGEST WALKING ROBOT
FANNY

Fanny is a massive 26-foot-high, 51-foot-long, fire-breathing dragon. She is also the world's biggest walking robot. In 2012, a German company designed and built Fanny using both hydraulic and electronic parts. She is radio remote-controlled with nine controllers, while 238 sensors allow the robot to assess her environment. She does this while walking on her four legs or stretching wings that span 39 feet. Powered by a 140-horsepower diesel engine, Fanny weighs a hefty 24,250 pounds—as much as two elephants—and breathes real fire using 24 pounds of liquid gas.

FANNY STATS

09/27/2012 Date of Fanny's launch

26'10" Fanny's height in feet and inches

51'6" Fanny's length in feet and inches

12' Fanny's body width in feet

39' Fanny's wingspan in feet

ALMOST HUMAN! In Hangzhou Zoo, China, a Malayan sun bear stood on its hind legs and looked to all the world like a human in a bear suit. A video of the bear went viral, forcing the zoo to proclaim the creature really was an animal. The species is the smallest bear in the world, weighing 60–150 pounds, but it has the longest tongue—nearly 10 inches long—which allows it to get at honey and burrowing insects. In the wild, a mother bear sometimes picks up a cub in her "arms" and walks upright on her hind legs, just like a human.

BIRD OF THE CENTURY The puteketeke—also known as the Australasian crested grebe—was the winner of New Zealand's Bird of the Century contest, which was held for the first time in 2023. The event marked the centenary of the annual Bird of the Year contest, organized by the conservation group Forest and Bird. Aided by a campaign by British American comedian John Oliver, the puteketeke received an overwhelming 290,374 votes from 195 countries, putting the second-place kiwi, New Zealand's national bird, in the shade with only 12,904 votes.

SEALS WHO SURF Seals are playful creatures and it is not uncommon to see them leaping onto surfboards once in a while (pictured). In 2023, however, one particular enthusiast became a frequent visitor. The baby harbor seal—known locally as Sammy—started joining the early morning surfers in San Diego to take up his favorite position on the front of a long board. He's a natural nose-rider!

WOLVERINE SPOTTED The wolverine—the largest land-dwelling member of the weasel family—disappeared from California in 1922, so spotting one in the eastern Sierra Nevada mountains in 2023 was a real surprise! It's thought the lone wanderer ambled in from a neighboring population in the Rocky Mountains, possibly due to high levels of snow in the highlands during 2023. The new arrival was only the second to be seen in the state for over a hundred years.

SPLOOTING SQUIRRELS In the summer of 2023, a video of a splooting squirrel posted on Facebook in June by the Texas Parks and Wildlife Department prompted a flurry of photos of furry animals in similar poses. Lying spread-eagled on their belly is what some creatures do to keep cool in hot weather. And with temperatures reaching 100°F in July, who can blame them?

KOALA

Australia's koala sleeps for up to twenty hours a day and still manages to look sleepy when awake. This is due to the koala's unbelievably monotonous diet. It feeds, mostly at night, on the aromatic leaves of eucalyptus trees. The leaves have little nutritional or caloric value, so the marsupial saves energy by snoozing. It jams its rear end into a fork in the branches of its favorite tree so that it cannot fall out while asleep.

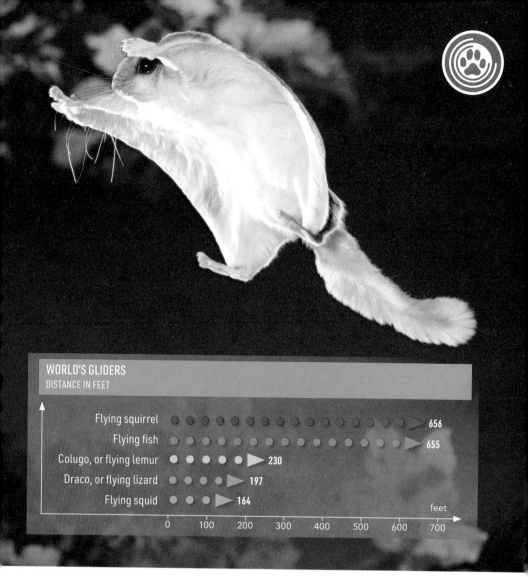

WORLD'S GLIDERS
DISTANCE IN FEET

		feet
Flying squirrel	⦾⦾⦾⦾⦾⦾⦾⦾⦾⦾⦾⦾⦾⦾⦾⦾⦾⦾▷	**656**
Flying fish	⦾⦾⦾⦾⦾⦾⦾⦾⦾⦾⦾⦾⦾⦾⦾⦾⦾⦾▷	**655**
Colugo, or flying lemur	⦾⦾⦾⦾⦾▷	**230**
Draco, or flying lizard	⦾⦾⦾⦾▷	**197**
Flying squid	⦾⦾⦾▷	**164**

0   100   200   300   400   500   600   700

WORLD'S BEST GLIDER
FLYING SQUIRREL

Flying squirrels are champion animal gliders. The Japanese giant flying squirrel has been scientifically recorded making flights over distances of up to 164 feet from tree to tree. These creatures have been estimated to make 656-foot flights when flying downhill. The squirrel remains aloft using a special flap of skin on either side of its body, which stretches between its wrist and ankle. Its fluffy tail acts as a stabilizer to keep it steady, and the squirrel changes direction by twisting its wrists and moving its limbs.

AFRICAN BUSH ELEPHANT
WORLD'S **HEAVIEST** LAND ANIMAL

The African bush elephant is the world's largest living land animal. The biggest known bush elephant stood 13.8 feet at the shoulder and had an estimated weight of 13.5 tons. The African bush elephant is also the animal with the largest outer ears. The outsize flappers help keep the animal cool on the open savanna. The Asian elephant has much smaller earflaps because it lives in the forest and is not exposed to the same high temperatures.

This little critter, the Kitti's hog-nosed bat, measures just 1.3 inches long, with a wingspan of 6.7 inches, and weighs 0.07–0.10 ounces. It's tied for first place as the world's smallest mammal with Savi's Etruscan shrew, which is longer at 2.1 inches but lighter at 0.04–0.06 ounces. The bat lives in west-central Thailand and southeast Myanmar, and the shrew is found in areas from the Mediterranean to Southeast Asia.

WORLD'S TINIEST BAT
KITTI'S HOG-NOSED BAT

WORLD'S LARGEST PRIMATE
GORILLA

The largest living primates on Earth are the eastern gorillas, and the biggest subspecies among them is the very rare mountain gorilla. The tallest known was an adult male silverback, named for the color of the fur on his back. He stood 6.4 feet tall, but he was an exception—silverbacks generally grow no bigger than 5.9 feet tall. Gorillas have long arms. The record holder had an arm span measuring 8.9 feet, while adult male humans have an average arm span of just 5.9 feet.

The male mandrill's face is as flamboyant as his rear end. The vivid colors of both are brightest at breeding time. The colors announce to his rivals that he is an alpha male and he has the right to breed with the females. His exceptionally long and fang-like canine teeth reinforce his dominance. The mandrill is the world's largest monkey, as well as the most colorful.

WORLD'S MOST COLORFUL MONKEY
MANDRILL

CHEETAH

WORLD'S FASTEST LAND ANIMAL

The fastest reliably recorded running speed of any animal was that of a zoo-bred cheetah that reached an incredible 61 miles per hour on a flat surface. The record was achieved in 2012 from a standing start by a captive cheetah at the Cincinnati Zoo. More recently, wild cheetahs have been timed while actually hunting their prey in the bush in Botswana. Using GPS technology and special tracking collars, the scientists found that these cheetahs had a top speed of 58 miles per hour over rough terrain.

FASTEST LAND ANIMALS
TOP SPEED

Cheetah — 61 mph
Ostrich — 60 mph
Pronghorn — 55 mph
Springbok — 55 mph
Lion — 30 mph

miles per hour

0   10   20   30   40   50   60

There are only five big cats that roam Earth: tiger, lion, jaguar, leopard, and snow leopard. The biggest and heaviest is the Siberian, or Amur, tiger, which lives in the taiga (boreal forest) of eastern Siberia, where it hunts deer and wild boar. The largest reliably measured tigers have been about 11.8 feet long and weighed around 705 pounds, but there have been claims of larger individuals, such as the male shot in the Sikhote-Alin Mountains in 1950. That tiger weighed 847 pounds.

WORLD'S LARGEST BIG CAT TIGER

GIRAFFE
WORLD'S TALLEST LIVING ANIMAL

Giraffes living on the savannas of eastern and southern Africa are the world's tallest animals. The tallest known bull giraffe measured 19 feet from the ground to the top of his horns. He could have peered into the upstairs window of a two-story house. Despite having much longer necks than we do, giraffes have the same number of neck vertebrae. They also have long legs, with which they can either speedily escape from predators or kick them to keep them away.

GIRAFFE STATS

6 FEET Height of a calf at birth

25 YEARS Average lifespan

100 POUNDS Adult's daily food consumption of leaves and twigs

WORLD'S NOISIEST LAND ANIMAL
HOWLER MONKEY

The howler monkeys of Latin America are deafening. Males have an especially large hyoid bone. This horseshoe-shaped bone in the neck creates a chamber that makes the monkeys' deep guttural growls sound louder for longer. It is said that their calls can be heard up to 3 miles away. Both males and females call, and they holler mainly in the morning. It is thought that these calls are often one troop of monkeys telling neighboring troops where they are.

On Australia's Great Barrier Reef, and off the coasts of Indonesia and Papua New Guinea, lives a member of the carpet shark family that can walk! Called the epaulette shark, it is recognizable by a black spot, edged in white, on either side of its body. No more than 3 feet long, it lives in the intertidal zone, and when the tide goes out, it is often left stranded in a rock pool. As the temperature of the water rises in the heat, oxygen levels sink. But when oxygen levels get too low for the shark to survive, it uses its paddle-shaped pectoral fins to pull itself over the rocks from one pool to the next, until it finds one with more oxygen in the water.

THE ONLY SHARK KNOWN TO WALK ON LAND
EPAULETTE SHARK

NARWHAL

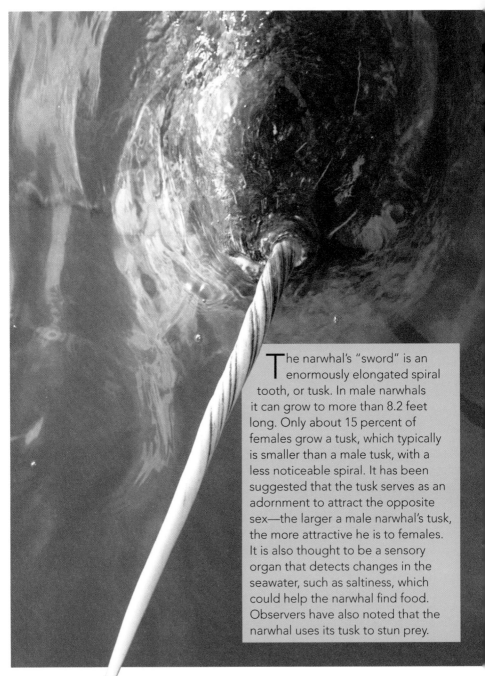

The narwhal's "sword" is an enormously elongated spiral tooth, or tusk. In male narwhals it can grow to more than 8.2 feet long. Only about 15 percent of females grow a tusk, which typically is smaller than a male tusk, with a less noticeable spiral. It has been suggested that the tusk serves as an adornment to attract the opposite sex—the larger a male narwhal's tusk, the more attractive he is to females. It is also thought to be a sensory organ that detects changes in the seawater, such as saltiness, which could help the narwhal find food. Observers have also noted that the narwhal uses its tusk to stun prey.

Blue whales are truly colossal. The largest one accurately measured was 110 feet long, and the heaviest weighed 209 tons. They feed on tiny krill, which they filter from the sea. On land, the largest known animal was a titanosaur—a huge dinosaur that lived 101 million years ago in what is now Argentina. A skeleton found in 2014 suggests the creature was 121 feet long and weighed 77 tons. It belonged to a young titanosaur, so an adult may have been bigger than a blue whale.

THE WORLD'S LARGEST LIVING ANIMAL

BLUE WHALE

WORLD'S BIGGEST FISH
WHALE SHARK

Recognizable from its spotted skin and enormous size, the whale shark is the world's largest living fish. It grows to a maximum length of about 66 feet. Like the blue whale, this fish feeds on some of the smallest creatures: krill, marine larvae, small fish, and fish eggs. The whale shark is also a great traveler. One female was tracked swimming 4,800 miles from Mexico—where hundreds of whale sharks gather each summer to feed—to the middle of the South Atlantic Ocean, where it is thought she may have given birth.

The great white shark is considered the animal most likely to make an unprovoked attack on people. Of the 949 shark attacks recorded over the last 400 years, 351 have been attributed to great whites—fifty-nine of them fatal. The biggest reliably measured great white was 21 feet long, making it the largest predatory fish in the sea. Its jaws are lined with 3-inch-long, triangular, serrated teeth that can slice through flesh, sinew, and even bone. Of the sixty-nine unprovoked shark attacks in 2023, ten were fatal. Three of these were caused by great whites. Humans are not this creature's food of choice; they don't have enough fat on their bodies. White sharks prefer blubber-rich seals and dolphins. It is likely that many of the attacks on people are probably cases of mistaken identity.

SHARK BITES GREAT WHITE SHARK

WORLD'S LARGEST LIZARD KOMODO DRAGON

There are dragons on Indonesia's Komodo Island, and they're dangerous. The Komodo dragon's jaws are lined with sixty replaceable, serrated, backward-pointing teeth. Its saliva is laced with deadly bacteria and venom that the dragon works into a wound, ensuring its prey will die quickly. Because this is the world's largest lizard, prey can be as big as a pig or a deer. It can grow up to 10.3 feet long and weigh 366 pounds.

WORLD'S DEADLIEST FROG
POISON DART FROG

A poison dart frog's skin exudes toxins. There are several species, and the more vivid a frog's color, the more deadly its poison. The skin color warns potential predators that the frogs are not good to eat, although one animal—the fire-bellied snake—is immune to the chemicals and happily feeds on these creatures. It is thought that the frogs do not manufacture their own poisons, but obtain the chemicals from their diet of ants, millipedes, and mites. The most deadly species to humans is also the largest: Colombia's golden poison dart frog. At just 1 inch long, a single frog has enough poison to kill ten to twenty people.

SALTWATER
CROCODILE

The saltwater crocodile, or "saltie," is the world's largest living reptile. Males can grow to over 20 feet long, but a few old-timers become real monsters. A well-known crocodile in the Segama River, Borneo, left an impression on a sandbank that measured 33 feet. The saltie can be found in areas from eastern India to northeastern Australia, where it lives in mangroves, estuaries, and rivers. It is sometimes found out at sea. The saltie is an ambush predator, grabbing any animal that enters its domain—including humans. Saltwater crocodiles account for twenty to thirty attacks on people per year, up to half of which are fatal.

WORLD'S SMALLEST REPTILE NANO-CHAMELEON

In a mountain forest in northern Madagascar lives the smallest known reptile in the world: the nano-chameleon *Brookesia nana*. From his snout to the tip of his tail, the male of the species is just 0.85 inches long—roughly the length of a sunflower seed. The female is a little longer: 1.14 inches. They live among the leaf litter on the forest floor, where they hunt for mites and springtails. They are well camouflaged with a light-brown-and-gray body, and they hide from predators among blades of grass. Unlike most chameleons, they do not change color, but they do have the chameleon's long, extendable tongue to capture prey.

HOATZIN

The hoatzin eats leaves, flowers, and fruit. It ferments the food in its crop (a pouch in its esophagus). This habit leaves the bird with a foul odor, which has led people to nickname the hoatzin the "stinkbird." About the size of a pheasant, this bird lives in the Amazon and Orinoco river basins of South America. A hoatzin chick has sharp claws on its wings, like a pterodactyl. If threatened by a snake, the chick jumps from the nest into the water, using its wing claws to help it climb back up.

The ribbon-tailed astrapia has the longest feathers in relation to body size of any wild bird. The male, which has a beautiful, iridescent blue-green head, sports a pair of white ribbon-shaped tail feathers that are more than 3.3 feet long—three times the length of its 13-inch-long body. It is one of Papua New Guinea's birds of paradise and lives in the mountain forests of central New Guinea, where males sometimes have to untangle their tails from the foliage before they can fly.

BIRD WITH THE LONGEST TAIL

RIBBON-TAILED ASTRAPIA

BALD EAGLE

With a wingspan of more than 6.6 feet, bald eagles need space to land and take off—so their nests can be gargantuan. Over the years, a nest built by a pair of bald eagles in St. Petersburg, Florida, has taken on epic proportions. Measuring 9.5 feet across and 20 feet deep, it is made of sticks, grass, and moss. At one stage, it was thought to have weighed at least 2 tons, making it the largest nest ever constructed by a pair of birds. Although one pair nests at a time, these huge structures are often the work of several pairs of birds, each building on top of the work of their predecessors.

The African ostrich lays the largest eggs of any living bird, yet they are the smallest eggs relative to the size of the mother's body. Each egg is some 5.9 inches long and weighs about 3.5–5 pounds, while the mother is about 6.2 feet tall and the father is about 7.8 feet tall, making the ostrich the world's largest living bird. The female lays about fifty eggs per year, and each egg contains as much yolk and albumen as twenty-four hens' eggs. It takes an hour to soft-boil an ostrich egg!

WORLD'S LARGEST BIRD EGG AFRICAN OSTRICH EGG

WORLD'S BIGGEST PENGUIN
EMPEROR
PENGUIN

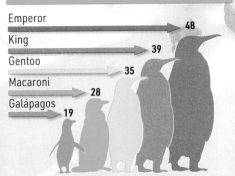

EMPEROR PENGUIN STATS

80 POUNDS Average weight of an adult

1,751 FEET Depth to which an adult can swim

22 MINUTES Length of time an adult can stay underwater

FIVE OF THE WORLD'S PENGUINS
HEIGHT IN INCHES

Emperor — 48
King — 39
Gentoo — 35
Macaroni — 28
Galápagos — 19

At 4 feet tall, the emperor penguin is the world's biggest living penguin. It has a most curious lifestyle, breeding during the long, dark Antarctic winter. The female lays a single egg and carefully passes it to the male. She then heads out to sea to feed, while he remains with the egg balanced on his feet and tucked under a fold of blubber-rich skin. There he stands with all the other penguin dads, huddled together to keep warm in the blizzards and 100-mile-per-hour winds that scour the icy continent. Come spring, the egg hatches, the female returns, and Mom and Dad swap duties, taking turns feeding and caring for their fluffy chick.

WORLD'S HEAVIEST SPIDER
GOLIATH BIRD-EATING
TARANTULA

The size of a dinner plate, the female goliath bird-eating tarantula has a leg span of 11 inches and weighs up to 6.17 ounces. This is the world's heaviest spider and a real nightmare for an arachnophobe (someone with a fear of spiders). Its fangs can pierce a person's skin, but its venom is no worse than a bee sting. The hairs on its body are more of a hazard. When threatened, it rubs its abdomen with its hind legs and releases tiny hairs that cause severe irritation to the skin. Despite its name, this spider does not actually eat birds very often.

At 2 inches long, with a ¼-inch stinger and fearsome jaws, the Asian giant hornet is more than twice the size of other hornet species. While native to Asia, this hornet is also known in the Pacific Northwest. Preying on honeybees, a swarm of giant hornets can wipe out an entire hive in only a couple of hours. This is a problem for farmers, whose crops need honeybees to pollinate them. In the Pacific Northwest, for example, honeybees are crucial to the successful harvest of cherries, apples, and blueberries. Thankfully, the hornet nests are a rare sight in the United States and farmers are developing ways to protect their bees.

WORLD'S BIGGEST HORNET ASIAN GIANT HORNET

DRACULA ANT

The Dracula ant, *Mystrium camillae*, of tropical areas of Africa, Southeast Asia, and Australasia, makes the fastest movement of any known animal on Earth. In the time it takes you to blink, it can open and close its jaws *five thousand* times. It does this by pressing its jaws together, storing energy like a spring, and then sliding them past each other at up to 200 miles per hour. Such fast jaws allow the ant to stun or kill its prey, such as fast-moving centipedes, which have their own formidable jaws!

DESERT LOCUST

WORLD'S **FASTEST** FLYING INSECT

Flying insects are difficult to clock, and many impressive speeds have been claimed over the years. The fastest airspeed reliably timed was by fifteen desert locusts that managed an average of 21 miles per hour. Airspeed is the actual speed at which the insect flies. It is different from ground speed, which is often enhanced by favorable winds. A black cutworm moth whizzed along at 70 miles per hour while riding the winds ahead of a cold front. The most shocking measurement, however, is that of a horsefly with an estimated airspeed of 90 miles per hour while chasing an air-gun pellet! Understandably, this is one speed that has not been verified!

MOSQUITO

Female mosquitoes live on the blood of birds and mammals—humans included. However, the problem is not what they take, but what they leave behind. In some mosquitoes' saliva are organisms that cause the world's most deadly illnesses, including malaria, yellow fever, dengue fever, West Nile virus, and encephalitis. It is estimated that mosquitoes transmit diseases to 700 million people every year, of which 725,000 die. In 2021, the World Health Organization (WHO) announced the release of a vaccine that can help prevent a mosquito-borne disease called malaria, and that has the potential to save tens of thousands of lives.

Each year, millions of dragonflies fly thousands of miles across the Indian Ocean from South India to East Africa. Most of them are globe skimmers, a species known to fly long distances and at altitudes up to 3,280 feet. They can travel 2,175 miles in 24 hours. Coral cays on the way have little open fresh water, so the insects stay there for a few days before moving on to East Africa. There, they follow the rains, at each stop taking advantage of temporary rainwater pools to lay their eggs to hatch where their young can rapidly develop. Four generations are involved in a round trip of about 11,000 miles—farther than the distance from New York City to Sydney.

WORLD'S LONGEST INSECT MIGRATION GLOBE SKIMMER

LOST CAT FOUND A woman and her partner were mountain biking in Oregon when they heard that their house in Juneau, Alaska, had been washed away by floods from the Mendenhall Glacier. They lost all their possessions, including their cat, Leo. Twenty-six days later, the woman spotted a photo of Leo on social media, where Juneau residents were trying to connect strays with their owners. She went to investigate, called the cat's name, and out trotted Leo! The resourceful cat had somehow survived the devastation.

BULL ON THE HIGHWAY Drivers passing through Norfolk, Nebraska, in August 2023 could be forgiven for thinking they were hallucinating. There on the highway, riding shotgun in a Ford Crown Victoria sedan, was a 2,200-pound bull of immense proportions, all the way down to his gigantic horns. The animal was Howdy Doody, a mixed Watusi-longhorn steer that, according to his owner, Lee Meyer, enjoys riding in his specially modified car.

WORLD'S OLDEST CAT DOOR? This cat-sized hole at the base of a door at Exeter Cathedral, Devon, UK, dates to around 1598. Records show the bishop paid carpenters to carve the hole in an old door so the resident tabby could come and go at will. The door leads to the mechanism driving an astronomical clock that was lubricated by animal fat. This attracted mice, and the hole may have been created so the cat could control the vermin.

MAINE'S CANINE LIFEGUARDS Buoy and Beacon are lifeguards at Scarborough Beach State Park, Maine, but they do not wear swimsuits or sunscreen! They are both Newfoundland dogs, a breed known for its ability to swim well. With some training, they help keep beaches safe. They are second responders; if a swimmer's in trouble, a human first responder leaps into action, while the dog heads out into the surf (along with another human and rescue equipment). Then the dog helps haul them all back to shore.

SNOOPY LOOK-ALIKE With more than one million likes on Instagram, a post on the Doodle Dogs Club account shows a photo of Bayley, a cute sheepadoodle, who bears more than a passing resemblance to Snoopy, the dog from the cartoon *Peanuts*. From a most perfect button nose to long floppy ears, and a black patch on his back, one-year-old Bayley is the spitting image of Charlie Brown's pet pooch.

WORLD'S FLUFFIEST RABBIT ANGORA RABBIT

In most people's opinion, the Angora rabbit is the world's fluffiest bunny. The breed originated in Turkey and is thought to be one of the world's oldest rabbit breeds as well. It became popular with the French court in the mid-eighteenth century. Today, it is bred for its long, soft wool, which is shorn every three to four months. One of the fluffiest bunnies ever was buff-colored Franchesca, owned by English Angora rabbit expert Dr. Betty Chu. In 2014, Franchesca's fur was measured at 14.37 inches, a world record that has yet to be beaten.

Originally bred in Argentina, the Falabella miniature horse is the world's smallest recognized breed of horse. While newborn foals can be 12–22 inches tall at the withers (the ridge between the shoulder blades), adults mature at 25–34 inches. They are proportionally similar to other horses, and not ponies, except they are tiny; and they have seventeen vertebrae in their backbone rather than the usual eighteen. Bay (brown body with a black mane and tail) and black are the most common colors, but there are pintos, palominos, and spotted individuals resembling Appaloosas.

LITTLEST HORSE BREED
FALABELLA

WORLD'S HAIRIEST DOG
KOMONDOR

The world's hairiest dog breed is the Komondor, or Hungarian sheepdog. It is a powerful dog that was bred originally to guard sheep. Its long, white, dreadlock-like "cords" enable it not only to blend in with the flock but also to protect itself from bad weather and bites from wolves. This is a large dog, standing over 27.5 inches at the shoulders. Its hairs are up to 10.6 inches long, giving it the heaviest coat of any dog.

AMERICA'S MOST POPULAR DOGS

1. French Bulldog
2. Labrador Retriever
3. Golden Retriever
4. German Shepherd Dog
5. Poodle
6. Dachshund
7. Bulldog
8. Beagle
9. Rottweiler
10. German Shorthaired Pointer

AMERICA'S MOST POPULAR DOG BREED FRENCH BULLDOG

According to the American Kennel Club, the French Bulldog remained the club's favorite dog breed for the second year running in 2023. Known affectionately as the "Frenchie," this cute, playful little dog is a bulldog in miniature, right down to the wrinkled face, snub nose, and "bat" ears. In 2022, the Frenchie brought an end to the Labrador Retriever's reign as the country's no. 1 breed, which lasted an incredible thirty-one years. It looks as if the adorable little bulldog is here to stay!

WORLD'S LONGEST-LIVED LAND ANIMAL

JONATHAN

Having celebrated his 190th birthday in 2022, Jonathan the tortoise is believed to be the world's longest-lived land animal. He hatched around 1832 on the Aldabra Atoll, part of the Seychelles archipelago in the Indian Ocean. Since 1882, he's been living on a distant island in another ocean—St. Helena, part of a British overseas territory in the South Atlantic—where he was presented to the governor at the time as a gift. Today, he lives on the lawn in front of Plantation House, the official residence of the governor of St. Helena, with three other giant tortoises. Jonathan puts his longevity down to a healthy diet of fresh grass and fruit.

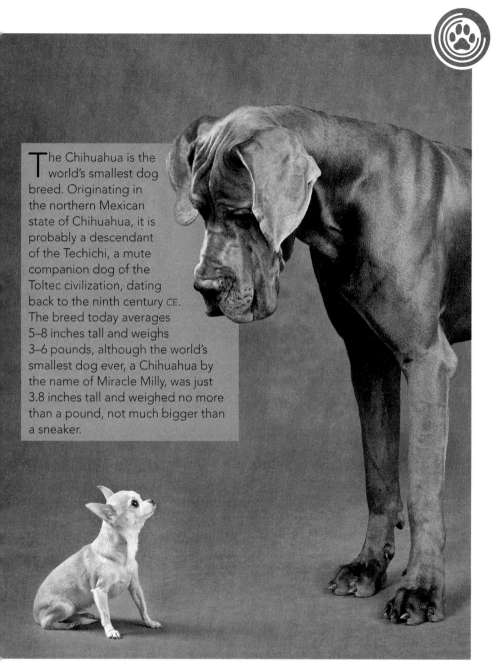

The Chihuahua is the world's smallest dog breed. Originating in the northern Mexican state of Chihuahua, it is probably a descendant of the Techichi, a mute companion dog of the Toltec civilization, dating back to the ninth century CE. The breed today averages 5–8 inches tall and weighs 3–6 pounds, although the world's smallest dog ever, a Chihuahua by the name of Miracle Milly, was just 3.8 inches tall and weighed no more than a pound, not much bigger than a sneaker.

WORLD'S SMALLEST DOG BREED
CHIHUAHUA

RAGDOLL
WORLD'S MOST POPULAR CAT BREED

In February 2024, the Cat Fanciers' Association announced that the Ragdoll was the world's most popular cat breed. This was the fifth year running that the "Raggie" had taken the top spot as the most registered cat breed of the previous year. With its lush, silky fur and big blue eyes, this is a cat that loves to be around human beings, relaxing like a "rag doll" when curled up on your lap. The year's listings also saw the Persian rise from fifth place to third and the Siberian rise from tenth place to ninth.

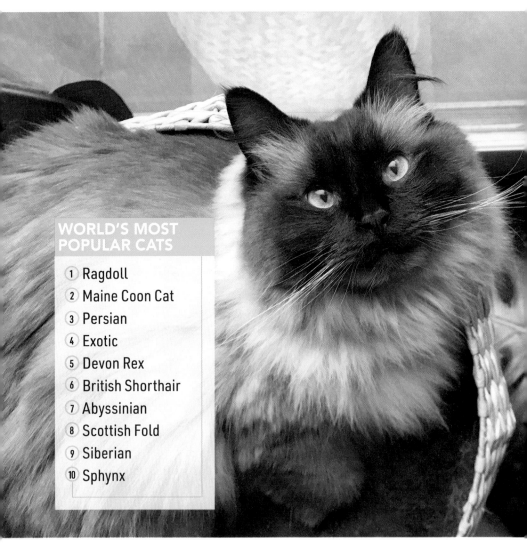

WORLD'S MOST POPULAR CATS

1. Ragdoll
2. Maine Coon Cat
3. Persian
4. Exotic
5. Devon Rex
6. British Shorthair
7. Abyssinian
8. Scottish Fold
9. Siberian
10. Sphynx

The Sphynx breed of cats is famous for its wrinkles and the lack of a normal coat, but it is not entirely hairless. Its skin is like the softest chamois leather, but it has a thin layer of down. It behaves more like a dog than a cat, greets its owners when they come home, and is friendly to strangers. The breed originated in Canada, where a black-and-white cat gave birth to a hairless kitten called Prune in 1966. Subsequent breeding gave rise to the Sphynx.

WORLD'S
BALDEST CAT SPHYNX

incredible earth trending

MONTH OF CLIMATE CHAOS In July 2023, extreme weather hit every continent on Earth. The extent of Antarctica's sea ice was the lowest on record, due to high temperatures. North America, South America, and Africa saw record heat and drought. In Asia, deadly floods and landslides hit India, Pakistan, and other countries. China recorded its highest temperature ever—125.9°F. Europe's temperatures also soared, with its second warmest year on record, reaching highs of 118°F. Wildfires raged across parts of North America, scorching millions of acres in Canada alone.

GHOST LAKE REAPPEARS Tulare Lake once covered nearly 800 square miles in California's San Joaquin Valley. In the 1800s, settlers drained the lake, dammed the rivers that flowed into it, and used the fertile land for farming cotton, pistachios, and other crops. During 2023, the lake reappeared for the first time in years. Heavy rainfall and record melting snow filled about 178 square miles of the lake bed as of June.

THIRSTY CACTI Record-breaking heat in 2023 took its toll on Arizona's iconic saguaro cacti. These desert plants thrive in hot, dry conditions. They are slow growing, can live for 150 to 175 years, and reach heights of 40 feet! However, the cacti rely on summer monsoon rains and cooler night temperatures to stay healthy. Without enough water or relief from the heat, they shrivel up. During 2023, the city of Phoenix, Arizona, was over 110°F for thirty-one consecutive days, and some of the tall, stately plants collapsed.

SUPERCHARGED STORM The eruption of a massive underwater volcano in Tonga, in the South Pacific, culminated on January 15, 2022, sparking a record-breaking lightning storm. Hunga Tonga-Hunga Ha'apai's volcanic plume shot at least 36 miles into the sky above sea level. For about 11 hours, the storm raged, producing almost 200,000 lightning flashes. At its most intense period, there were 2,615 flashes per minute.

CLIMATE ACTION A landmark agreement was reached at the 2023 United Nations Climate Change Conference (COP 28) in Dubai, United Arab Emirates, with nations around the world agreeing to move away from fossil fuels. Calling on nations to cut greenhouse gas emissions, with a target of net-zero emissions by 2050, the deal builds on the 2015 Paris Agreement, which aimed to limit Earth's temperature to 2.7°F above preindustrial levels.

BRISTLECONE PINE

An unnamed bristlecone pine in the White Mountains of California is the world's oldest continuously standing tree. It is 5,071 years old, beating its bristlecone rivals the Methuselah (4,865 years old) and Prometheus (4,853 years old). Sweden is home to an even older tree, a Norway spruce (which are often used as Christmas trees) that took root about 9,555 years ago. However, this tree has not been standing continuously. It is long-lived because it can clone itself. When the trunk dies, a new one grows up from the same rootstock. In theory, it could live forever.

WORLD'S TALLEST TREES
HEIGHT IN FEET

feet

Tree	Height
California redwood, California, US	379.1
Mountain ash, Styx Valley, Tasmania	327.4
Coast Douglas-fir, Oregon, US	327.3
Sitka spruce, California, US	317.0
Giant sequoia, California, US	314.0

A coast redwood named Hyperion is the world's tallest known living tree. It is 379.1 feet tall, and could have grown taller if a woodpecker had not hammered its top. It's growing in a remote part of the Redwood National and State Parks in Northern California, but its exact location is kept a secret for fear that too many visitors would upset its ecosystem. It is thought to be 700–800 years old.

WORLD'S TALLEST TREE CALIFORNIA
REDWOOD

WORLD'S LARGEST FRUIT
PUMPKIN

Pumpkins are known for being large fruits, but with a bit of horticultural nudging they can grow to be truly monstrous. Gourd-grower Travis Gienger's latest colossal triumph proved this point at the 2023 World Championship Pumpkin Weigh-Off held in Half Moon Bay, California. Weighing in at a record-breaking 2,749 pounds, the pumpkin was heavier than a small family car. Grown from a 2365 Wolf seed (a new type known for yielding especially large pumpkins), and dubbed "Michael Jordan" due to its resemblance to a basketball, the pumpkin was big enough to make more than 650 pies.

The leaf of the giant Amazon water lily can grow as wide as 8.6 feet across. It has an upturned rim and a waxy, water-repellent upper surface. On the underside of the leaf is a riblike structure that traps air, enabling the leaf to float easily. The ribs are also lined with sharp spines that protect them from aquatic plant eaters. A full-grown leaf is so large and so strong that it can support up to 99 pounds in weight.

GIANT AMAZON
WORLD'S TOUGHEST LEAF WATER LILY

HANG SON DOONG,
VIETNAM

Measuring 1.35 billion cubic feet, Hang Son Doong, in Vietnam, is the world's largest cave by volume. It was first discovered in 1991 by an elderly man collecting firewood, and he later revealed its location to a British caving expedition. When the explorers lit up the cave with their powerful lamps, they discovered caverns of immense size. In one, a jumbo jet could sit comfortably on the floor, with room to spare, and you could have fit in a tall skyscraper, too. The explorers went on to discover the world's tallest stalagmites—up to 250 feet tall—and a 300-foot-high calcite wall, which they nicknamed the "Great Wall of Vietnam."

HANG SON DOONG STATS

MOUNTAIN RIVER CAVE Name's meaning

1991 Year of discovery

5.6 MILES Total length

1.35 BILLION CUBIC FEET Total volume

GARDEN OF EDAM

At two points in the vast cave system, explorers found that the roof had collapsed and light spilled in, forming a huge circular hole, or doline. The largest of the two dolines, the Garden of Edam, features a tropical rainforest in the center of the cave, with some trees 100 feet tall and inhabitants that include lizards, birds, and monkeys.

THE DEEPEST POINT ON LAND
DENMAN GLACIER

The deepest point on land has been discovered under the Denman Glacier in East Antarctica. Deep below the Antarctic ice sheet, which is 1.3 miles thick, on average, there is an ice-filled canyon whose floor is 11,500 feet below sea level. By comparison, the lowest clearly visible point on land is in the Jordan Rift Valley, on the shore of the Dead Sea, just 1,412 feet below sea level. It makes the Denman canyon the deepest canyon on land. Only trenches at the bottom of the ocean are deeper. The floor of the deepest trench—the Mariana Trench—is close to 7 miles below the sea's surface.

GEYSER FIELDS
NUMBER OF GEYSERS

Yellowstone, Idaho/Montana/Wyoming, US
540

Valley of Geysers, Kamchatka, Russia
139

El Tatio, Andes, Chile
84

Orakei Korako, New Zealand
33

Hveravellir, Iceland
16

geysers

| 0 | 150 | 250 | 400 | 550 |

YELLOWSTONE NATIONAL PARK
WORLD'S GREATEST NUMBER OF GEYSERS

There are about 1,000 geysers that erupt worldwide, and 540 of them are in Yellowstone National Park, US. That's the greatest concentration of geysers on Earth. The most famous is Old Faithful, which spews out a cloud of steam and hot water to a maximum height of 185 feet every 44 to 125 minutes. Yellowstone's spectacular water display is due to its closeness to molten rock from Earth's mantle that rises up to the surface. One day the park could face an eruption 1,000 times as powerful as that of Mount St. Helens in 1980.

EARTH'S TALLEST MOUNTAIN ABOVE SEA LEVEL
MOUNT EVEREST

Mount Everest has grown. In December 2020, Nepal and China agreed on an official height that is 2.8 feet higher than the previous calculation. The mega mountain is located in the Himalayas, on the border between Tibet and Nepal. The mountain acquired its official name from surveyor Sir George Everest, but local people know it as Chomolungma (Tibet) or Sagarmatha (Nepal). In 1953, Sir Edmund Hillary and Tenzing Norgay were the first people to reach its summit. Now more than 650 people per year manage to make the spectacular climb.

WORLD'S TALLEST MOUNTAINS
HEIGHT ABOVE SEA LEVEL IN FEET

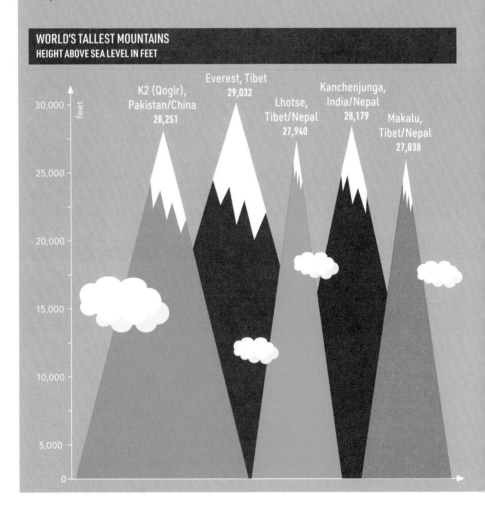

K2 (Qogir), Pakistan/China — 28,251
Everest, Tibet — 29,032
Lhotse, Tibet/Nepal — 27,940
Kanchenjunga, India/Nepal — 28,179
Makalu, Tibet/Nepal — 27,838

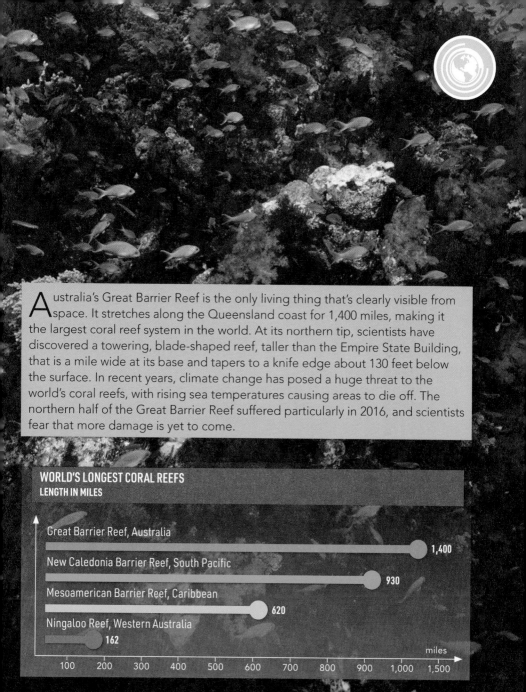

Australia's Great Barrier Reef is the only living thing that's clearly visible from space. It stretches along the Queensland coast for 1,400 miles, making it the largest coral reef system in the world. At its northern tip, scientists have discovered a towering, blade-shaped reef, taller than the Empire State Building, that is a mile wide at its base and tapers to a knife edge about 130 feet below the surface. In recent years, climate change has posed a huge threat to the world's coral reefs, with rising sea temperatures causing areas to die off. The northern half of the Great Barrier Reef suffered particularly in 2016, and scientists fear that more damage is yet to come.

WORLD'S LONGEST CORAL REEFS
LENGTH IN MILES

Reef	Length (miles)
Great Barrier Reef, Australia	1,400
New Caledonia Barrier Reef, South Pacific	930
Mesoamerican Barrier Reef, Caribbean	620
Ningaloo Reef, Western Australia	162

miles: 100 200 300 400 500 600 700 800 900 1,000 1,500

WORLD'S LONGEST CORAL REEF SYSTEM
GREAT BARRIER REEF

SAHARA DESERT

Sahara means simply "great desert," and great it is. It's the largest hot desert on the planet. It's almost the same size as the United States or China and dominates North Africa from the Atlantic Ocean in the west to the Red Sea in the east. This desert is extremely dry, with most of the Sahara receiving less than 0.1 inch of rain a year, and some places getting none at all for several years. It is stiflingly hot, up to 122°F, making this one of the hottest and driest regions in the world.

WORLD'S LARGEST HOT DESERTS
SIZE IN SQUARE MILES

Sahara Desert, North Africa — **3.63 million**

Arabian Desert, Western Asia — **900,000**

Great Victoria Desert, Australia — **250,000**

Kalahari Desert, Africa — **220,000**

Syrian Desert, Western Asia — **190,000**

sq miles

0   500,000   1 million   4 million

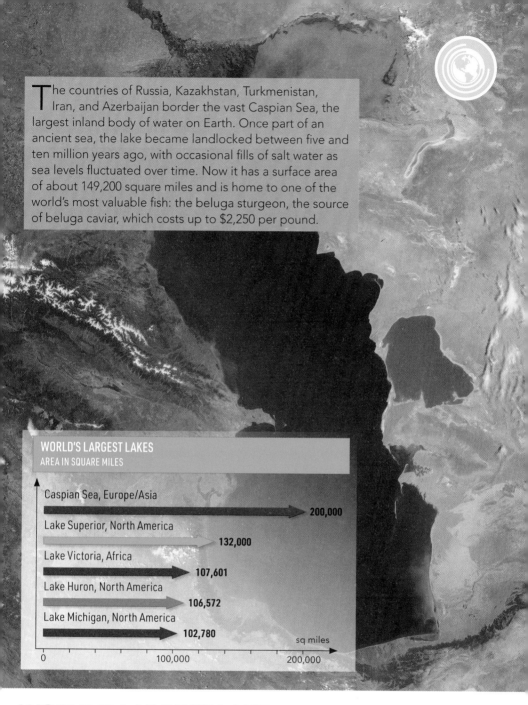

The countries of Russia, Kazakhstan, Turkmenistan, Iran, and Azerbaijan border the vast Caspian Sea, the largest inland body of water on Earth. Once part of an ancient sea, the lake became landlocked between five and ten million years ago, with occasional fills of salt water as sea levels fluctuated over time. Now it has a surface area of about 149,200 square miles and is home to one of the world's most valuable fish: the beluga sturgeon, the source of beluga caviar, which costs up to $2,250 per pound.

WORLD'S LARGEST LAKES
AREA IN SQUARE MILES

Caspian Sea, Europe/Asia — **200,000**

Lake Superior, North America — **132,000**

Lake Victoria, Africa — **107,601**

Lake Huron, North America — **106,572**

Lake Michigan, North America — **102,780**

sq miles

0   100,000   200,000

WORLD'S **LARGEST** LAKE
CASPIAN SEA

WORLD'S LONGEST RIVER
NILE RIVER

Flowing from south to north through eastern Africa, the Nile River is the world's longest. It begins in rivers that flow into Lake Victoria, which borders modern-day Uganda, Tanzania, and Kenya. One of those rivers is the Kagera River. From the lake, the Nile proper heads north across eastern Africa for 4,132 miles to the Mediterranean. Its water is crucial to people living along its banks. They use it to irrigate precious crops, generate electricity, and, in the lower reaches, as a river highway.

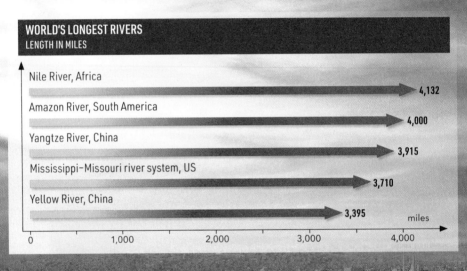

WORLD'S LONGEST RIVERS
LENGTH IN MILES

Nile River, Africa	4,132
Amazon River, South America	4,000
Yangtze River, China	3,915
Mississippi–Missouri river system, US	3,710
Yellow River, China	3,395

miles

0   1,000   2,000   3,000   4,000

LARGEST WAVE SURFED NAZARÉ

The town of Nazaré in Portugal is wide open to Atlantic Ocean swells. It's famous for the mountainous surf that makes landfall there, and it's one of the most sought-after destinations for champion surfers. So it's no surprise that German-born and Hawaii-trained Sebastian Steudtner rode the highest wave ever recorded there. Aided by the seafloor topography and the direction of the wind, the wave rose to a massive 86 feet, enabling Steudtner to claim the world record for surfing "the largest wave." He achieved a near-perfect ride, staying ahead of the curling wave immediately behind him and exiting gently to one side before the gigantic wall of water came crashing down.

WILDFIRES

The summer of 2023 was plagued by extensive wildfires. Sparked by lightning, discarded cigarette butts, abandoned but still smoldering campfires, sparks from braking trains and off-road vehicles, and land clearance that got out of control, the fires devastated communities across the Northern Hemisphere. Many people lost their homes and livelihoods, and some lost their lives.

CANADA

Canada has great swathes of forest, stretching across the country from the Pacific to the Atlantic. During long, hot summers, when the trees and brush have dried out, all it takes is a bolt of lightning to ignite the wood. In 2023, wildfires raged through forests in British Columbia, Alberta, Quebec, and Nova Scotia, the worst wildfire season on record. Smoke from fires in the east blanketed New York City and reached all the way to Scandinavia.

HAWAII

On the Hawaiian island of Maui, almost all of the historic town of Lahaina was reduced to ash by a fast-moving wildfire fueled by strong winds and dry conditions. Miraculously, one house was left standing, mostly untouched, after the rest were destroyed in the conflagration. At least ninety-nine people lost their lives.

2023

RHODES, EUROPE

The Mediterranean is no stranger to wildfires. They occur frequently during the summer, but they are usually contained by local fire crews. What happened on the Greek island of Rhodes on July 23, however, was on a different scale. Large parts of the island were ablaze, and private boats and coast guard vessels had to evacuate trapped residents and tourists from beaches.

LA PALMA, CANARY ISL.

About 18 square miles of pine forests in the north of the island went up in flames, and at least 4,000 people were evacuated from their homes. Especially hot weather and strong winds fanned the flames, with the same heat wave roasting parts of North America and southern Europe.

BATAGAIKA CRATER, SIBERIA

WORLD'S LARGEST PERMAFROST CRATER

There is a huge gash in the permafrost of Siberia. Local people know it as the "gateway to the underworld," but to Russian geologists it is the Batagaika Crater, the largest permafrost crater in the world. At nearly 2 miles long and half a mile across at the widest point, the crater is visible from space. It has appeared because the permafrost—normally permanently frozen soil—is thawing. The effects of climate change are causing the ice that keeps the soil solid to melt, and the meltwater is washing the soil away, forming "slumps." Categorized as a mega-slump, Batagaika Crater is enlarging at a rate of about 100 feet per year.

0.5 MILES

2 MILES

In February 2022, the World Meteorological Organization (WMO) announced a new record for the world's longest single lightning flash, which it had discovered by scanning satellite imagery. The strike occurred two years earlier, on April 29, 2020. In the event, a 477.2-mile-long megaflash of lightning ripped through the skies above Mississippi, Louisiana, and Texas—quite a record, given that strikes rarely stretch over 10 miles. The megaflash was just 36 miles longer than the previous record holder, a 440.6-mile-long strike in Brazil on October 31, 2018.

LONGEST LIGHTNING FLASH
UNITED STATES

HOTTEST MONTH EVER
JULY 2023

It's official: July 2023 was the hottest month ever. Scientists from NASA's Goddard Institute for Space Studies declared that "July 2023 was hotter than any other month in the global temperature record." Globally, July was 0.43°F warmer than any July in NASA's records. That might not sound like much, but when you compare the temperature against the July average between 1951 and 1980, the 2023 temperature was 2.1°F warmer. NASA's data reveals that the five hottest Julys since 1880, when records began, have all occurred in the past five years. The record-breaking July 2023 is part of a continuing trend of warming from greenhouse gas emissions caused by humans.

The greatest depth of snow on record in the United States occurred at Tamarack, near the Bear Valley ski resort in California, on March 11, 1911. The snow reached an incredible 37.8 feet deep. Tamarack also holds the record for the most snowfall in a single month, with 32.5 feet in January 1911. Mount Shasta, California, had the most snowfall in a single storm, with 15.75 feet falling during February 13–19, 1959. The most snow in twenty-four hours was a snowfall of 6.3 feet at Silver Lake, Colorado, on April 14–15, 1921.

CALIFORNIA AND COLORADO

MOST SNOWFALL IN THE UNITED STATES

WORLD'S **LARGEST** HAILSTONE
SOUTH DAKOTA

In August 2010, the town of Vivian, South Dakota, was bombarded by some of the biggest hailstones ever to have fallen out of the sky. They went straight through roofs of houses, smashed car windshields, and stripped vegetation. Among them was a world record breaker, a hailstone the size of a volleyball. It was 8 inches in diameter and weighed 2.2 pounds.

Mawsynram is a cluster of villages in the Khasi Hills of India. The plateau on which they sit overlooks the vast flatlands of Bangladesh. With 467.4 inches of rain falling each year, on average, Mawsynram is considered to be the wettest place on Earth. Life here is not without its problems. Wooden bridges are washed away frequently, so locals build living bridges of knotted and interwoven roots of Indian rubber trees. Some people use a traditional "knup" umbrella in the heavy rains. Woven from reeds, this keeps the whole body dry.

WORLD'S WETTEST PLACE
MAWSYNRAM

BUG-ZAPPING UMBRELLA In 2023, New Jersey teenager Selina Zhang invented a gadget that combats the much talked about spotted lanternfly. This invasive species is thought to have come to the US from China in a shipment of stone around ten years ago. Now present in seventeen US states, the creatures pose a serious threat to agriculture. They feed on the sap of some seventy plant species, leaving a sticky excretion that inhibits photosynthesis. Making use of a patio umbrella, Zhang's invention, ArTreeficial, is an AI-driven, solar-powered "tree" that lures, traps, and zaps the bugs in an electronic mesh.

FOURTH GRADER CREATES STATE COOKIE Fourth graders at a Montgomery, Alabama, school competed to create a state cookie. Mary Claire Cook won the competition in June 2023, which was judged by older students at the school. The Yellowhammer cookie is made with pecans, peanut butter, honey, and oats—ingredients associated with the state. "Yellowhammer" is the nickname for the state bird, the northern flicker.

RARE BISON BORN Wyoming Hope, an American bison, gave birth in May 2023. Even though she is white, there was no guarantee her calf would have the same coloring, but it did! The white fur comes from cattle genes. In the late 1800s, ranchers kept herds of bison and cattle together. Sacred to many Native American communities, the white bison is a symbol of hope. According to the National Bison Association, the birth of a white bison is a 1-in-10-million event.

DIAMOND DISCOVERY In September 2023, Aspen Brown was on a birthday treasure hunt when she spotted something glittering in a large rock. It turned out to be a 2.95-carat golden-brown diamond. The seven-year-old was visiting Arkansas's Crater of Diamonds State Park, which sits in the crater left behind by a volcanic eruption about 100 million years ago. The eruption brought gem-studded rocks to the surface. Many of the park's visitors find small diamonds and other gems, but Brown's diamond is a rare discovery.

BOLD NEW DESIGN FOR STATE FLAG Minnesota picked a new flag in December 2023. The left side of the flag features a white star set against a K-shaped block of navy blue. This is a nod to Minnesota's boundary shape and its motto, *L'étoile du Nord* (Star of the North). On the right, a block of light blue represents water. Minnesota contains more than 10,000 lakes. The flag is based on the winning submission by twenty-four-year-old Minnesotan writer and artist Andrew Prekker.

STATE WITH THE OLDEST MARDI GRAS CELEBRATION
ALABAMA

French settlers held the first American Mardi Gras in Mobile, Alabama, in 1703. Yearly celebrations continued until the Civil War and began again in 1866. Today, around one million people gather in the city during the vibrant two-week festival. Dozens of parades with colorful floats and marching bands wind through the streets each day. Partygoers attend masked balls and other lively events sponsored by the city's social societies. On Mardi Gras, which means "Fat Tuesday" in French, six parades continue the party until the stroke of midnight, which marks the end of the year's festivities and the beginning of Lent.

STATE WITH THE **MOST NATIVE AMERICANS** PER CAPITA

ALASKA

With a total population of 734,000 people and a Native American population exceeding 115,000, Alaska is the state with the highest number of Native Americans per capita—nearly one in six. Alaska is also the state with the highest number of tribal areas, having more than 200 Native villages in total. Among the great Indigenous tribes of Alaska are the Aleut, the Yup'ik, the Eyak, and the Inuit. While most live in modern communities, each tribe continues to uphold the traditions of its elders.

LARGEST DAM IN THE US
ARIZONA

The state of Arizona is home to the nation's largest dam by volume, an honor it shares with Nevada, since the dam straddles the state border. Finished in 1935, the Hoover Dam was a massive feat of engineering that took around 21,000 people to build; it stands at an amazing 726.4 feet from the rocky bottom to the road over the top. The Hoover Dam is a concrete arch-gravity dam, which means it controls the movement of the water both through its arch shape, pointing upstream, and the use of gravity. The dam not only controls the flow of the mighty Colorado River, but also generates a huge amount of hydroelectric power as it does so—enough for more than 1.3 million people.

ARKANSAS

ONLY STATE WHERE DIAMONDS ARE MINED

Crater of Diamonds, near Murfreesboro, Arkansas, is the only active public diamond mine in the United States. Farmer and former owner John Wesley Huddleston first discovered diamonds there in August 1906, and a diamond rush overwhelmed the area after he sold the property to a mining company. For a time, there were two competing mines in this area, but in 1969 General Earth Minerals bought both mines to run them as private tourist attractions. Since 1972, the land has been owned by the state of Arkansas, which designated the area as Crater of Diamonds State Park. Visitors can pay a fee to search through plowed fields in the hope of discovering a gem for themselves.

STATE WITH THE LARGEST NATURAL AMPHITHEATER
CALIFORNIA

Almost one hundred years since it first opened its doors to the public, the Los Angeles Hollywood Bowl remains the largest natural outdoor amphitheater in the country. The summer home of both the Los Angeles Philharmonic and the Hollywood Bowl Orchestra has a capacity for approximately 17,000 people. Many bring picnics and blankets to make the most of their music-filled summer evenings under the stars. Several events have drawn record crowds, including The Beatles, who attracted 18,700 fans in 1964, and Chris Tomlin, whose 2019 performance was a sellout. The highest attendance record of all time goes to the French singer Lily Pons, whose 1936 performance drew an incredible 26,410 people.

COLORADO

STATE WITH THE **LARGEST ELK** POPULATION

Colorado is currently home to around 280,000 elk, making it the state with the largest elk population. Elk live on both public and private land across the state, from the mountainous regions to lower terrain. Popular targets for hunting, these creatures are regulated by both the Colorado Parks and Wildlife department and the National Park Service. Many elk live within the boundaries of Colorado's Rocky Mountain National Park. Elk are among the largest members of the deer family, and the males—called bulls—are distinguishable by their majestic antlers.

CONNECTICUT

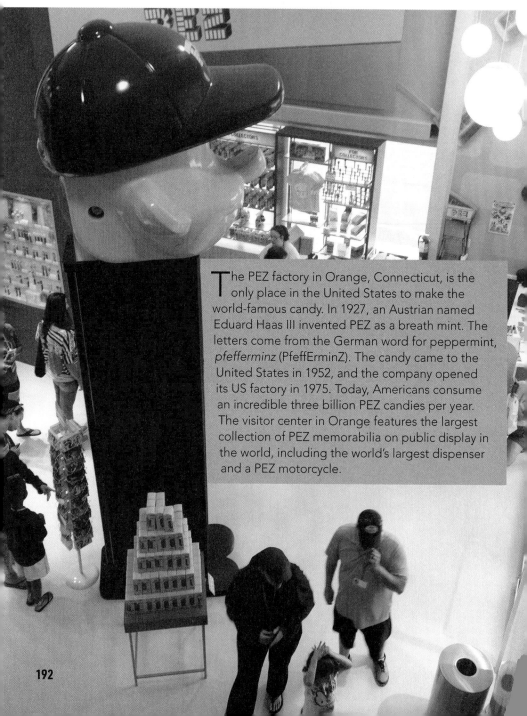

The PEZ factory in Orange, Connecticut, is the only place in the United States to make the world-famous candy. In 1927, an Austrian named Eduard Haas III invented PEZ as a breath mint. The letters come from the German word for peppermint, *pfefferminz* (PfeffErminZ). The candy came to the United States in 1952, and the company opened its US factory in 1975. Today, Americans consume an incredible three billion PEZ candies per year. The visitor center in Orange features the largest collection of PEZ memorabilia on public display in the world, including the world's largest dispenser and a PEZ motorcycle.

STATE WITH THE MOST
HORSESHOE CRABS

DELAWARE

D elaware Bay has the largest American horseshoe crab (*Limulus polyphemus*) population in the world. These creatures can be seen in large numbers on the bay's beaches in the spring. They appear during high tides on new and full moons, when they come onto land to spawn (deposit eggs). Horseshoe crabs have changed very little in the past 250 million years and have, therefore, been called living fossils. It is impossible to know the exact number of horseshoe crabs in the region, so every spring, volunteers at some of the state's beaches conduct counts to track spawning activity. The most recent Delaware Bay Horseshoe Crab Survey reported an estimated 1.4 million horseshoe crabs on the state's Delaware Bay shoreline in 2022.

FLORIDA

ONLY STATE IN WHICH ALLIGATORS AND CROCODILES LIVE SIDE BY SIDE

Where else but Everglades National Park might you expect to see both alligators and crocodiles living in the wild? The alligator is the more common of the two in America. According to the Florida tourist office, "If you don't see one during an Everglades visit, you're doing something wrong." The American crocodile is endangered, and so a rarer find. Both species like to bask in the sun on the banks of mangrove swamps and other bodies of water. The best way to tell the difference between the two is to check the shape of the snout. An alligator has a more U-shaped snout; a crocodile's is shaped more like a V. And did you know? Not only is Florida the only *state* where you can see alligators and crocodiles, it's also the only place in the *world*!

STATE WITH THE LARGEST SPORTS HALL OF FAME

GEORGIA

At 43,000 square feet, Georgia's Sports Hall of Fame honors the state's greatest sports stars and coaches. The museum includes 14,000 square feet of exhibition space and a 205-seat theater. It owns more than 3,000 artifacts and memorabilia from Georgia's professional, college, and amateur athletes. At least 1,000 of these artifacts are on display at any time. The Hall of Fame corridor features over 400 inductees, such as golf legend Bobby Jones, baseball hero Jackie Robinson, and Olympic track medalist Wyomia Tyus.

HAWAII

Iolani Palace in downtown Honolulu is the only official royal residence in the United States. The palace was built during 1879–1882 by King Kalakaua, inspired by the grand castles of Europe. The monarchs did not live there for long, however. In 1893, the Kingdom of Hawaii was overthrown by US forces. Kalakaua's sister, Queen Liliuokalani, was even held prisoner in the palace in 1895 following a plot to put her back on the throne. Restored to its nineteenth-century condition, Iolani Palace is now open to the public as a museum.

IDAHO

FIRST STATE WITH A
BLUE FOOTBALL FIELD

Boise State's Albertsons Stadium, originally dubbed the "Smurf Turf" and now nicknamed "The Blue," was the first blue football field in the United States. In 1986, when the time came to upgrade the old turf, athletics director Gene Bleymaier realized that they would be spending a lot of money on the new field, yet most spectators wouldn't notice the difference. So he asked AstroTurf to create the new field in the school's colors. Since the field's creation, students at the school have consistently voted for blue turf each time the field has been upgraded. Today, nine teams play on a colored playing field, including the Coastal Carolina Chanticleers, whose teal field is dubbed the "Surf Turf."

STATE WITH THE OLDEST FREE PUBLIC ZOO
ILLINOIS

Lincoln Park Zoo, in Chicago, Illinois, remains the oldest free public zoo in the United States. Founded in 1868—just nine years after the Philadelphia Zoo, the country's oldest zoo overall—Lincoln Park Zoo does not charge admission fees. More than two-thirds of the money for the zoo's operating budget comes from food, retail, parking, and fundraisers. Nonetheless, the zoo continues to grow. In October 2021, it opened a new exhibit—the Pepper Family Wildlife Center— a savanna-style habitat that is home to a pride of African lions.

INDIANA
FIRST PROFESSIONAL
BASEBALL LEAGUE GAME

On May 4, 1871, the first National Association professional baseball league game took place on Hamilton Field in Fort Wayne, Indiana. The home team, the Kekiongas, took on the Forest Citys of Cleveland, beating them 2–0 against the odds. The Kekiongas were a little-known team at the time. In fact, the first National Association game had been scheduled to take place between two better-known teams, the Washington Olympics and the Cincinnati Red Stockings in Washington, DC, on May 3. Heavy rain forced a cancellation, however, and so history was made at Fort Wayne the following day.

IOWA

STATE WITH THE SHORTEST, STEEPEST RAILROAD

At 296 feet long, Fenelon Place Elevator in Dubuque, Iowa, is the shortest railroad in the United States, and its elevation of 189 feet also makes it the steepest. In 1882, businessman and former mayor J. K. Graves hired John Bell to build the railway. Graves lived at the top of the Mississippi River bluff and wanted a quicker commute down into the town below. Today's railway, modernized in 1977, is open to the public. It costs $2 for an adult one-way trip and consists of two house-shaped cars traveling in opposite directions on parallel tracks.

KANSAS

ONLY TALLGRASS PRAIRIE NATIONAL PARK

At just 60 miles wide, Flint Hills, Kansas's Tallgrass Prairie National Preserve, is the only US national park dedicated to this ecosystem. Due to plowing by farmers who use the fertile ground to plant crops, the ecosystem is in danger of disappearing worldwide. It has survived in Flint Hills partly because the landscape is not suitable for plowing. The tallgrass prairie contains more than 500 plant species, including different types of grasses—notably Indian grass and big bluestem. In 2009, bison were reintroduced to the preserve in Kansas, and the herd has since grown to about 100 strong.

KENTUCKY

The Kentucky Derby is the longest-running sporting event in the United States. It's also accompanied by the biggest fireworks display held annually in the United States—"Thunder Over Louisville"—which kicks off the racing festivities. Zambelli Fireworks, the display's creator, says that the show requires nearly 60 tons of fireworks shells and a massive 700 miles of wire cable to sync the fireworks to music. The theme for the 2023 show was "Through the Decades," a fabulous celebration of the most memorable Thunder moments over the years.

STATE WITH THE MOST CRAWFISH
LOUISIANA

The majority of the crawfish consumed in the United States are caught in the state of Louisiana. While these critters may look like tiny lobsters, crawfish are actually freshwater shellfish and are abundant in the mud of the state's bayous—sometimes they are called "mudbugs." Before white settlers arrived in Louisiana, crawfish were a favorite food of the Native tribes, who caught them using reeds baited with venison. Today, crawfish are both commercially farmed and caught in their natural habitat. The industry currently yields more than 100 million pounds of crawfish a year, and the crustaceans are an integral part of the state's culture, with backyard crawfish boils remaining a popular local tradition.

STATE WITH THE
OLDEST STATE FAIR

MAINE

In January 1819, the Somerset Central Agricultural Society sponsored the first-ever Skowhegan State Fair. In the 1800s, state fairs were important places for farmers to gather and learn about new agricultural methods and equipment. After Maine became a state in 1820, the fair continued to grow in size and popularity, gaining its official name in 1942. Today, the Skowhegan State Fair welcomes more than 7,000 exhibitors and 100,000 visitors. Enthusiasts can watch events that include livestock competitions, tractor pulling, a demolition derby, and much more during the ten-day show.

MARYLAND

STATE WITH THE **OLDEST CAPITOL BUILDING**

The Maryland State House in Annapolis is both the oldest capitol building in continuous legislative use and the only statehouse to have once been used as the national capitol. The Continental Congress met there from 1783 to 1784, and it was where George Washington formally resigned as commander in chief of the army following the American Revolution. The current building is the third to be erected on that site and was actually incomplete when the Continental Congress met there in 1783, despite the cornerstone being laid in 1772. The interior of the building was finished in 1797, but not without tragedy—plasterer Thomas Dance fell to his death while working on the dome in 1793.

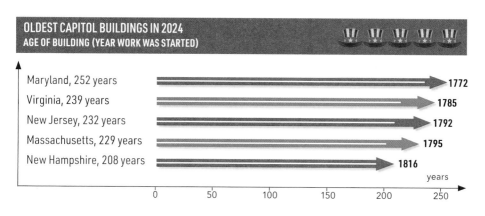

OLDEST CAPITOL BUILDINGS IN 2024
AGE OF BUILDING (YEAR WORK WAS STARTED)

State	Age	Year
Maryland, 252 years		1772
Virginia, 239 years		1785
New Jersey, 232 years		1792
Massachusetts, 229 years		1795
New Hampshire, 208 years		1816

years

0   50   100   150   200   250

MASSACHUSETTS

The first Thanksgiving celebration took place in 1621, in Plymouth, Massachusetts, when the Pilgrims and the Native Wampanoag people shared a feast. While the celebration became widespread in the Northeast in the late-seventeenth century, Thanksgiving was not celebrated nationally until 1863, when magazine editor Sarah Josepha Hale's writings convinced President Abraham Lincoln to make it a national holiday. Today, Plymouth, Massachusetts, holds a weekend-long celebration honoring its history: the America's Hometown Thanksgiving Celebration.

Michigan is home to more than 120 lighthouses! This is hardly surprising, given that Michigan is surrounded by four of the five Great Lakes and has about 3,288 miles of coastline. As many as 1,500 lighthouses were built in the United States—most of them in the early twentieth century. They are somewhat redundant today, because modern lighthouses now use technology to safely guide boats into harbors at night. But without these old lighthouses, many ships would have scuppered on the craggy rocks.

STATE WITH THE MOST LIGHTHOUSES
MICHIGAN

HALLOWEEN CAPITAL OF THE WORLD
MINNESOTA

The city of Anoka, Minnesota, proudly proclaims its title of Halloween Capital of the World. Anoka held its first celebration in 1920, when residents organized a costume parade and party, and it has gone all out for the spooky season ever since—except for two years during World War II. Now Halloween in Anoka is a month-long festival that includes the parade, a house-decorating contest, a "ghost run," and more. In 2022, Anoka fittingly made the news for being the home of the world's largest (and heaviest) jack-o'-lantern: Local pumpkin grower Travis Gienger's 2,560-pound creation was named Maverick and decorated with an eagle, inspired by the movie *Top Gun*.

Every four years, Jackson, Mississippi, hosts the USA International Ballet Competition, a two-week Olympic-style event that awards gold, silver, and bronze medals. The most recent one was held here in 2023. The competition began in 1964 in Varna, Bulgaria, and rotated among the cities of Varna; Moscow, Russia; and Tokyo, Japan. In June 1979, the competition came to the United States for the first time, and in 1982 Congress passed a joint resolution designating Jackson as the official home of the competition. Dancers vie for prizes and a chance to join ballet companies.

MISSISSIPPI

ONLY STATE TO HOLD THE INTERNATIONAL BALLET COMPETITION

MISSOURI
AMERICA'S FIRST ICE-CREAM CONE

It is said that America's first ice-cream cone was introduced through chance inspiration at the St. Louis World's Fair in 1904. According to the most popular story, a Syrian salesman named Ernest Hamwi saw that an ice-cream vendor had plenty of ice cream but not enough cups and spoons to serve it. Seeing that a neighboring vendor was selling waffle cookies, Hamwi took a cookie and rolled it into a cone for holding ice cream. An immediate success, Hamwi's invention was hailed by vendors as a "cornucopia"—an exotic word for a "cone."

MONTANA

STATE WITH THE MOST *T. REX* SPECIMENS

The first *Tyrannosaurus rex* fossil ever found was discovered in Montana—paleontologist Barnum Brown excavated it in the Hell Creek Formation in 1902. Since then, many major *T. rex* finds have been made in Montana—from the "Wankel Rex," discovered in 1988, to "Trix," unearthed in 2013, and "Tufts-Love Rex," discovered in 2016. This last was found about 20 percent intact at the site in the Hell Creek Formation. In recent years, a new exhibit named "Dinosaurs Under the Big Sky" has been installed in the Siebel Dinosaur Complex at the Museum of the Rockies in Bozeman, Montana. It is among the biggest and most updated dinosaur exhibits in the world.

LARGEST SAND DUNE FORMATIONS IN THE WESTERN HEMISPHERE
NEBRASKA

The Nebraska Sandhills is a vast sand dune formation that covers 19,300 square miles in the north-central part of the state—it makes up approximately one quarter of Nebraska's total land area. Some individual dunes stand up to 400 feet high and stretch as far as 20 miles. Unlike many sand dunes, Nebraska's are covered and stabilized by prairie grass, so they can be used to graze cattle. Around one third of Nebraska's beef cattle can be found here—that's more than half a million head! You won't find many people living in the Sandhills region, however—four of the ten least populated counties in the United States are located here, each with a population of less than one person per square mile.

NEVADA

STATE THAT PRODUCES THE MOST GOLD

Although it has been called the Silver State for its silver production, Nevada is also the state that produces the most gold. According to the Nevada Mining Association, Nevada produces more than three-quarters of America's gold and accounts for 3.7 percent of world gold production. Nevada's Carlin Trend is rich in gold deposits—and is, in fact, the world's second-largest gold resource. In 2020, two new gold deposits were found 20 miles west of Elko in the Ruby Valley. Once production starts, Nevada's gold output could rise by as much as five million ounces of gold over a decade.

NEW HAMPSHIRE

Nansen Ski Club, in Milan, New Hampshire, was founded by Norwegian immigrants in 1872, making it the oldest continuously operating skiing club in the United States. When it first opened, the venue accepted only other Scandinavians living in the area, but it was then made available to everyone as more skiing enthusiasts began to move into New Hampshire from Quebec to work in the mills there. For fifty years, the club was home to the largest ski jump east of the Mississippi, and the ski jump was used for Olympic tryouts.

STATE WITH THE **MOST DINERS**

NEW JERSEY

The state of New Jersey has more than five hundred diners, earning it the title of "Diner Capital of the World." The state has a higher concentration of diners than anywhere else in the United States. They are such an iconic part of the state's identity that, in 2016, a New Jersey diners exhibit opened at the Middlesex County Museum, showcasing the history of the diner, from early twentieth-century lunch cars to modern roadside spots. The state has many different types of diners, including famous restaurant-style eateries like Tops Diner in East Newark, as well as retro hole-in-the-wall diners with jukeboxes and booths.

STATE THAT MADE THE WORLD'S
LARGEST FLAT ENCHILADA
NEW MEXICO

New Mexico was home to the world's largest flat enchilada in October 2014, during the Whole Enchilada Fiesta in Las Cruces. The record-breaking enchilada measured 10.5 feet in diameter and required 250 pounds of masa dough, 175 pounds of cheese, 75 gallons of red chili sauce, 50 pounds of onions, and 175 gallons of oil. Led by Roberto's Mexican Restaurant, the making—and eating—of the giant enchilada was a tradition at the festival for thirty-four years before enchilada master Roberto Estrada retired in 2015.

AMERICA'S SMALLEST CHURCH

NEW YORK

The smallest church in America, Oneida's Cross Island Chapel, measures 81 by 51 inches and has just enough room for the minister and two churchgoers. Built in 1989, the church is in an odd location, in the middle of a pond. The simple, whitewashed clapboard chapel stands on a little jetty that has moorings for a boat or two. The island that the chapel is named for barely breaks the surface of the water nearby, and is simply a craggy pile of rock bearing a cross.

STATE WITH THE LARGEST PRIVATE HOUSE
NORTH CAROLINA

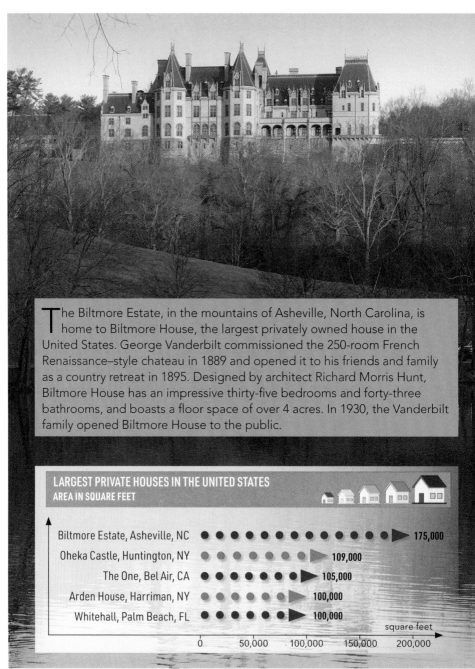

The Biltmore Estate, in the mountains of Asheville, North Carolina, is home to Biltmore House, the largest privately owned house in the United States. George Vanderbilt commissioned the 250-room French Renaissance–style chateau in 1889 and opened it to his friends and family as a country retreat in 1895. Designed by architect Richard Morris Hunt, Biltmore House has an impressive thirty-five bedrooms and forty-three bathrooms, and boasts a floor space of over 4 acres. In 1930, the Vanderbilt family opened Biltmore House to the public.

LARGEST PRIVATE HOUSES IN THE UNITED STATES
AREA IN SQUARE FEET

Biltmore Estate, Asheville, NC	175,000
Oheka Castle, Huntington, NY	109,000
The One, Bel Air, CA	105,000
Arden House, Harriman, NY	100,000
Whitehall, Palm Beach, FL	100,000

square feet

0   50,000   100,000   150,000   200,000

BIGGEST HONEY PRODUCER
NORTH DAKOTA

In the production of honey, North Dakota outstrips all other US states year after year. According to the USDA's National Agricultural Statistics Service, the state's 520,000 honey-producing colonies each yield an average 60 pounds of the sweet stuff per year. It seems the North Dakota climate is just right for honeybees and—more importantly—for the flowers from which they collect their nectar. Typical summer weather features warm days but cool nights.

OHIO FIRST LAWS PROTECTING WORKING WOMEN

I n the 1800s, working conditions in US factories were grueling and pay was very low. Most of the workers were women, and it was not uncommon for them to work for twelve to fourteen hours a day, six days a week. The factories were not heated or air-conditioned, and there was no compensation for being sick. By the 1850s, several organizations had formed to improve the working conditions for women and to shorten their workday. In 1852, Ohio passed a law limiting the working day to ten hours for women under the age of eighteen. It was a small step, but it was also the first act of legislation of its kind in the United States.

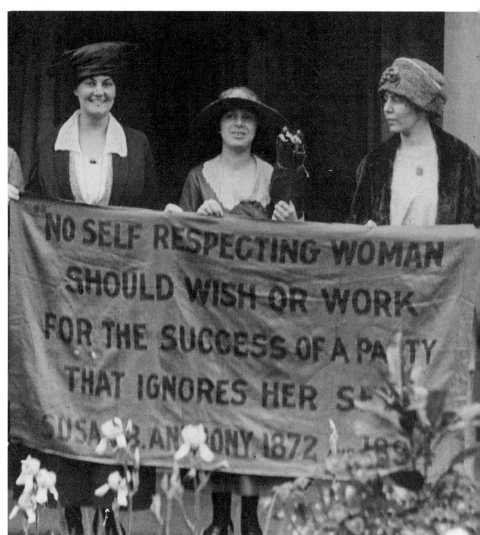

The Oklahoma State Capitol has one very unique feature: an oil well! Affectionately named "Petunia #1" because it was built by drilling at an angle through a flower bed, it was a working well from 1942 to 1986, producing more than 1.5 million barrels of oil by the time it dried up. The bottom of the well sits about 1.25 miles under the Capitol building, and visitors can see it as part of the Capitol tour. Petunia #1 was once one of more than twenty similar wells on Capitol grounds, which are situated on the Oklahoma City Oil Field, but its rig is now the only one to remain in place, preserved as a historic monument.

ONLY US STATE CAPITOL WITH AN OIL WELL BENEATH IT

OKLAHOMA

WORLD'S LARGEST OREGON
CINNAMON ROLL

Wolferman's Bakery holds the record for the largest cinnamon roll ever made. The spiced confection measured 9 feet long and was topped with 147 pounds of cream cheese frosting. It was made to celebrate the launch of the bakery's new 5-pound cinnamon roll. Using its popular recipe, Wolferman's needed 20 pounds of eggs, 350 pounds of flour, 378 pounds of cinnamon-sugar filling, and no fewer than 220 cinnamon sticks in their scaled-up version. The 1,150-pound cinnamon roll was transported to Medford's Annual Pear Blossom Festival in south Oregon, where visitors snapped it up for $2 a slice.

STATE THAT MANUFACTURES THE MOST CRAYONS

PENNSYLVANIA

Easton, Pennsylvania, is home to the Crayola crayon factory and has been the company's headquarters since 1976. The factory produces an amazing twelve million crayons every single day, made from uncolored paraffin and pigment powder. In 1996, the company opened the Crayola Experience in downtown Easton. The Experience includes a live interactive show during which guests can watch a "crayonologist" make crayons, just as they are made at the factory nearby.

STATE WITH THE OLDEST FOURTH OF JULY CELEBRATION
RHODE ISLAND

Bristol, Rhode Island, holds America's longest continuously running Fourth of July celebration. The idea for the celebration came from Revolutionary War veteran Rev. Henry Wight, of Bristol's First Congregational Church, who organized "Patriotic Exercises" to honor the nation's founders and those who fought to establish the United States. Today, Bristol begins celebrating the holiday on June 14, and puts on an array of events leading up to the Fourth itself—including free concerts, a baseball game, a Fourth of July Ball, and a half-marathon.

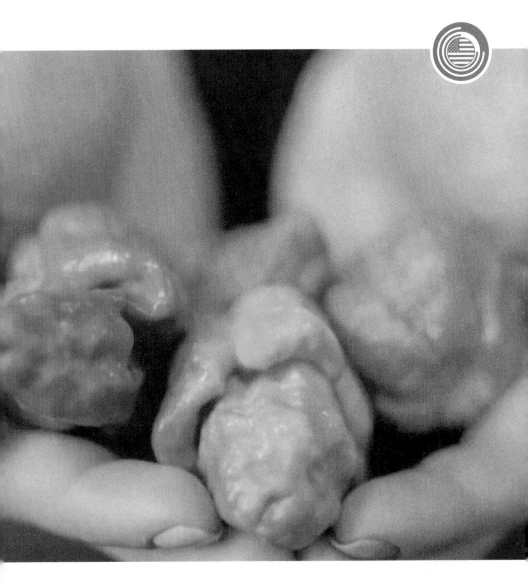

STATE WITH THE HOTTEST PEPPER
SOUTH CAROLINA

Entering the Guinness Book of World Records in August 2023, Pepper X, created by Smokin' Ed Currie of Rock Hill, South Carolina, is officially the hottest pepper in the world, measuring an average of 2.7 million Scoville heat units (SHU). To get a feel for how hot that is, just know that a regular jalapeño clocks in at 2,500–8,000 SHU. Currie also created a previous record holder, the Carolina Reaper, which held the record from 2013 to 2023, and measures an average of 1.64 million SHU.

STATE WITH THE LARGEST SCULPTURE
SOUTH DAKOTA

While South Dakota is famous as the home of Mount Rushmore, it is also the location of another giant mountain carving: the Crazy Horse Memorial. The mountain carving, which is still in progress, will be the largest sculpture in the world when it is completed, at 563 feet tall and 641 feet long. Korczak Ziolkowski, who worked on Mount Rushmore, began the carving in 1948 to pay tribute to Crazy Horse—the Lakota leader who defeated General Custer at the Battle of the Little Bighorn. More than seventy years later, Ziolkowski's family continues his work, relying completely on funding from visitors and donors.

TENNESSEE
STATE THAT MAKES ALL THE MOONPIES

Tennessee is the home of the MoonPie, which was conceived there in 1917 by bakery salesman Earl Mitchell, Sr., after a group of local miners asked for a filling treat "as big as the moon." Made from marshmallow, graham crackers, and chocolate, the sandwich cookies were soon being mass-produced at Tennessee's Chattanooga Bakery, and MoonPie was registered as a trademark by the bakery in 1919. MoonPies first sold at just five cents each and quickly became popular—even being named the official snack of NASCAR in the late 1990s. Today, Chattanooga Bakery makes around a million MoonPies every day.

LARGEST URBAN BAT COLONY
TEXAS

If you want to see a sky filled with hundreds of thousands of bats, head to Austin, Texas, anytime from mid-March to November. The city's Ann W. Richards Congress Avenue Bridge is home to the world's largest urban bat colony—roughly 1.5 million bats in all. The Mexican free-tailed bats first settled there in the 1980s, and numbers have grown steadily since. They currently produce around 750,000 pups per year. These days, the bats are a tourist attraction that draws about 140,000 visitors to the city, many of them hoping to catch the moment at dusk when large numbers of bats fly out from under the bridge to look for food.

UTAH
STATE WITH THE LARGEST SALTWATER LAKE

The Great Salt Lake, which inspired the name of Utah's largest city, is the largest saltwater lake in the United States, at around 75 miles long and 30 miles wide. Sometimes called "America's Dead Sea," it is typically larger than each of the states of Delaware and Rhode Island. Its size, however, fluctuates as water levels rise and fall. Since 1849, the water level has varied by as much as 23 feet, which can shift the shoreline by up to 15 miles. Great Salt Lake is too salty to support most aquatic life but is home to several kinds of algae, as well as the brine shrimp that feed on them.

STATE THAT PRODUCES
THE MOST MAPLE SYRUP
VERMONT

The state of Vermont produced 2.5 million gallons of maple syrup in 2022. The state's highest crop ever, it represents more than 50 percent of the country's total. Vermont's 1,500 maple syrup producers take sap from six million tree taps. They have to collect 40 gallons of maple sap in order to produce just 1 gallon of syrup. Producers also use maple sap for making other treats, such as maple butter, sugar, and candies.

VIRGINIA

FIRST STATE WITH A WOMAN-RUN BANK

In 1903, Maggie Lena Walker opened the St. Luke Penny Savings Bank in Richmond, making Virginia the first state with a bank founded and run by a woman. A leading civil activist, Walker was also Black, making her achievement all the more remarkable in a time when the Jim Crow laws did much to restrict the advancement of Blacks in the Southern states. Through the bank and other enterprises that included a newspaper and a department store, Walker sought to provide members of the Black community with opportunities to improve their lives through employment, investment, and supporting one another's businesses.

STATE WITH THE OLDEST GAS STATION
WASHINGTON

The Teapot Dome Service Station in Zillah, Washington, was once the oldest working gas station in the United States, and is still the only one built to commemorate a political scandal. Now preserved as a museum, the gas station was built in 1922 as a monument to the Teapot Dome Scandal, in which Albert Fall, President Warren G. Harding's secretary of the interior, took bribes to lease government oil reserves to private companies. The gas station, located on Washington's Old Highway 12, was moved in 1978 to make way for Interstate 82, then again in 2007 when the city of Zillah purchased it as a historic landmark.

STATE WITH THE LONGEST STEEL ARCH BRIDGE

WEST VIRGINIA

The New River Gorge Bridge in Fayetteville spans 3,030 feet and is 876 feet above the New River. It is both the longest and largest steel arch bridge in the United States. Builders used 88 million pounds of steel and concrete to construct it. The $37 million structure took three years to complete and opened on October 22, 1977. Bridge Day, held every October since 1980, is a BASE-jumping event at the New River Gorge Bridge. Hundreds of BASE jumpers and about 80,000 spectators gather for the one-day festival. Among the most popular events is the Big Way, in which large groups of people jump off the bridge together. During Bridge Day 2013, Donald Cripps became one of the world's oldest BASE jumpers, at eighty-four years old.

WORLD'S LARGEST AVIATION EVENT
WISCONSIN

Around 10,000 aircraft and more than 650,000 visitors flock to Oshkosh, Wisconsin, each summer for the Experimental Aircraft Association's annual AirVenture event at Wittman Regional Airport. In 2023, the event included nearly 1,500 vintage planes, more than 1,000 homemade planes, and more than 125 seaplanes and amphibious planes, among many other aircraft. The huge number of planes that fly in for this gathering together with AirVenture's daily air shows transform Wittman into the busiest airport in the world for around ten days each year, with nearly 150 takeoffs and landings per hour. The event began in 1953 and was originally held at Milwaukee's Curtiss-Wright Field, now known as Timmerman Airport. Oshkosh also is home to the EAA Aviation Museum.

STATE WITH THE LARGEST HOT SPRING

WYOMING

G rand Prismatic Spring, in Yellowstone National Park in Wyoming, is the largest hot spring in the United States. The spring measures 370 feet in diameter and is more than 121 feet deep; Yellowstone National Park says that the spring is bigger than a football field and deeper than a ten-story building. Grand Prismatic is not just the largest spring but also the most photographed thermal feature in Yellowstone due to its bright colors. The colors come from different kinds of bacteria, living in each part of the spring, that thrive at various temperatures. As water comes up from the middle of the spring, it is too hot to support most bacterial life, but as the water spreads out to the edges of the spring, it cools in concentric circles.

INSTAGRAM'S MOST-LIKED POST

Cristiano Ronaldo's high-profile transfer from English giant Manchester United to Saudi Arabia's Al Nassr in December 2022 sent shockwaves through the soccer world. It also generated enormous social media interest. After the Portuguese star was presented to the club's fans on January 3, 2023, Ronaldo's Instagram post commemorating the event attracted 27.9 million likes, making it the most-liked sporting Instagram post of 2023.

HIGHEST-PAID FEMALE SPORTS STAR

Serena Williams's trailblazing tennis career came to an end in 2022, but she hasn't stopped making headlines. In 2023, Williams remained the world's highest-paid female sports star, earning a staggering $45.3 million in mostly off-the-court endorsements. She was the only female athlete to appear in a list of sport's top fifty highest earners.

MOST-COVETED SPORTS KIT Lionel Messi's move to US Major League Soccer's Inter Miami in July 2023 sparked a never-before-seen rush from fans to buy his replica pink no. 10 jersey. As of October, Fanatics, a sports apparel company in the United States, had sold more Messi jerseys than that of any other athlete, with the exception of Philadelphia Eagles quarterback Jalen Hurts. At the start of 2024, it was the best-selling soccer shirt in North America.

FASTEST-GROWING SPORT Pickleball was named the fastest-growing sport in the United States for the third year in a row. Participation in the paddle sport, which combines elements of tennis, badminton, and Ping-Pong on a tennis-style court, almost doubled in 2022 and has grown an eye-opening 158.6 percent over the past three years.

SURPRISE NETFLIX SUCCESS Welsh soccer team Wrexham AFC was languishing in the semi-professional National League when, in February 2021, Hollywood stars Rob McElhenney and Ryan Reynolds took it over, promising to change its fortunes. They were true to their word: The club won promotion to the Football League in 2023, while an award-winning Netflix series, *Welcome to Wrexham*, saw it become one of the most talked-about teams in UK soccer. Social media interest in the team has risen by 921.23 percent since 2021.

DANNY WAY

WORLD'S LONGEST
SKATEBOARD RAMP JUMP

Many extreme sports activities are showcased at the annual X Games and Winter X Games. At the 2004 X Games, held in Los Angeles, skateboarder Danny Way set an amazing record that remains unbeaten. On August 8, Way made a long-distance jump of 79 feet, beating his own 2003 world record (75 feet). In 2005, he jumped over the Great Wall of China. He made the jump despite having torn ligaments in his ankle during a practice jump on the previous day.

WORLD'S HIGHEST TIGHTROPE WALK
FREDDY NOCK

Tightrope walking looks hard enough a few feet above the ground, but Swiss stuntman Freddy Nock took it to the next level when he walked between two mountains in the Swiss Alps in March 2015. On a rope set 11,590 feet above sea level, Freddy took about thirty-nine minutes to walk the 1,140 feet across to the neighboring peak. The previous record had been held since 1974, when Frenchman Philippe Petit walked between the Twin Towers of New York's former World Trade Center.

MOST SUCCESSFUL BMX RIDER OF ALL TIME
MAT HOFFMAN

No one has done more for the sport of BMX than Mat Hoffman. Nicknamed "The Condor," Hoffman is recognized as the greatest Vert rider in the sport, winning the World Vert Championship on ten occasions and also picking up six medals at the X Games. He is also credited with inventing more than 100 tricks, such as the 900 (which he successfully completed in 1989), a no-handed 900, a Flip Faki (a backflip that includes landing backward), and a Flair (a backflip with a 180-degree turn). He also holds the world record for the highest air achieved on a BMX bike over a 24-foot quarter bike (26.5 feet) and even took his bike BASE jumping off a 3,500-foot cliff in Norway.

WORLD'S HIGHEST BASKETBALL SHOT
DUDE PERFECT

On April 20, 2023, trick shooters Dude Perfect broke the world record for the highest-ever basketball shot, sinking it from a platform close to the top of iconic STRAT Tower on the Las Vegas Strip. Known locally as the Stratosphere, the tower is 1,149 feet tall, and Dude Perfect's platform was set at 856 feet above the basketball hoop, which was barely visible from above. The team spent twenty-five hours in total over a period of three days before Tyler Toney, one of the team's "dudes," achieved the record-breaking feat. Dude Perfect beat the previous world record—achieved by Australian team How Ridiculous in 2018—by 196 feet.

NBA CHAMPIONSHIP'S GREATEST RIVALRY
BOSTON CELTICS AND LA LAKERS

NBA CHAMPIONSHIP WINS		
LA Lakers	17	1949–2020
Boston Celtics	17	1957–2008
Golden State Warriors	7	1947–2022
Chicago Bulls	6	1991–1998
San Antonio Spurs	5	1999–2014

Between them, the LA Lakers and Boston Celtics have won almost half of the NBA Championship titles that have ever been played: seventeen each. The Celtics' best decade was the 1960s, when they won nine times, but the Lakers have arguably the better NBA record overall, with fourteen runner-up spots, compared to five for the Celtics. There have also been famous player rivalries, that of Larry Bird and Magic Johnson in the 1980s being perhaps the best known.

After a standout college career and three NCAA championships with the University of Connecticut Huskies, Diana Taurasi joined the Phoenix Mercury in the WNBA in 2004. Her prolific scoring helped the Mercury to its first WNBA title in 2007 (and two more since then), and her international career includes five consecutive Team USA Olympic golds, 2004–2020. Playing mainly as guard, Taurasi became the all-time leading WNBA scorer in 2017.

MOST CAREER POINTS IN THE WNBA Number of points	
Diana Taurasi	10,108
Tina Thompson	7,488
Tamika Catchings	7,380
Tina Charles	7,115
Candice Dupree	6,895
DeWanna Bonner	6,881

WNBA PLAYER WITH THE
MOST CAREER POINTS
DIANA TAURASI

FIRST NBA PLAYER TO REACH 40,000 CAREER POINTS

LEBRON JAMES

On Saturday, March 2, 2024, at age thirty-nine and sixty-two days, LeBron James became the first player in NBA history to reach 40,000 points, after having smashed Kareem Abdul-Jabbar's previous record of 38,387 in 2022. The milestone was set during a game against the Denver Nuggets, and the ball was taken out of play to preserve it for posterity. James's Los Angeles Lakers went on to lose the game 124–114, leaving him with "bittersweet" feelings over his achievement.

MOST CAREER POINTS IN THE NBA

LeBron James (2003–present)	40,017
Kareem Abdul-Jabbar (1969–1989)	38,387
Karl Malone (1985–2004)	36,928
Kobe Bryant (1996–2016)	33,643
Michael Jordan (1984–2003)	32,292

NBA ACCOLADES

LeBron James was named NBA Rookie of the Year in 2004. Since then, he has been voted the NBA's Most Valuable Player on four occasions, in 2009, 2010, 2012, and 2013.

JERRY RICE

Jerry Rice is generally regarded as the greatest wide receiver in NFL history. He played in the NFL for twenty seasons—fifteen of them with the San Francisco 49ers—and won three Super Bowl rings. As well as leading the career touchdowns list with 208, Rice also holds the "most yards gained" mark with 23,546 yards. Most of his touchdowns were from pass receptions (197), often working with the great 49ers quarterback Joe Montana.

NFL PLAYERS WITH THE MOST CAREER TOUCHDOWNS
Number of touchdowns (career years)

Jerry Rice	208	1985–2004
Emmitt Smith	175	1990–2004
LaDainian Tomlinson	162	2001–2011
Randy Moss	157	1998–2012
Terrell Owens	156	1996–2010

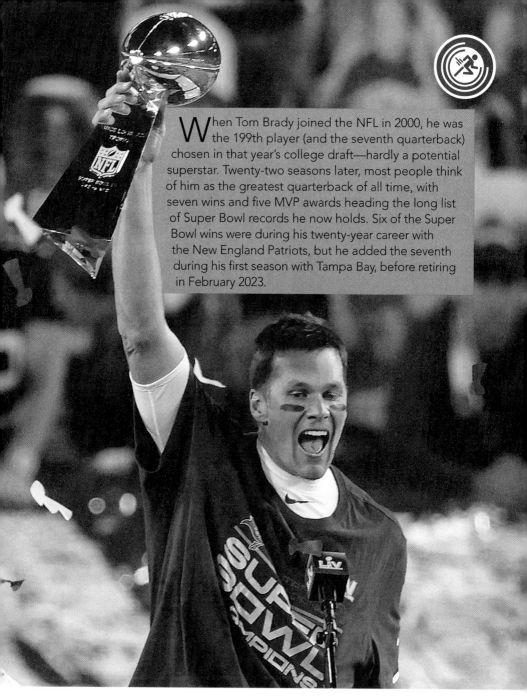

When Tom Brady joined the NFL in 2000, he was the 199th player (and the seventh quarterback) chosen in that year's college draft—hardly a potential superstar. Twenty-two seasons later, most people think of him as the greatest quarterback of all time, with seven wins and five MVP awards heading the long list of Super Bowl records he now holds. Six of the Super Bowl wins were during his twenty-year career with the New England Patriots, but he added the seventh during his first season with Tampa Bay, before retiring in February 2023.

TOM BRADY

PLAYER WITH THE MOST SUPER BOWL WINS

USC TROJANS

The Rose Bowl is college football's oldest postseason event, first played in 1902. Taking place near January 1 of each year, the game is normally played between the Pac-12 Conference champion and the Big Ten Conference champion, but one year in three it is part of college football's playoffs. The University of Southern California has easily the best record in the Rose Bowl, with twenty-five wins from thirty-four appearances, followed by the Ohio State Buckeyes (nine wins from sixteen appearances). The Buckeyes reached that second spot on the winners' list with their 48–45 victory over the Utah Utes on New Year's Day 2022.

WORLD SERIES WINS		
Number of wins		
New York Yankees	27	1923–2009
St. Louis Cardinals	11	1926–2011
Oakland Athletics *	9	1910–1989
Boston Red Sox **	9	1903–2018
San Francisco Giants ***	8	1905–2014

* Previously played in Kansas City and Philadelphia
** Originally Boston Americans
*** Previously played in New York

MLB TEAM WITH THE MOST WORLD SERIES WINS

NY YANKEES

The New York Yankees are far and away the most successful team in World Series history. Since baseball's championship was first contested in 1903, the Yankees have appeared forty times and won on twenty-seven occasions. The Yankees' greatest years were from the 1930s through the 1950s, when the team was led by legends such as Babe Ruth and Joe DiMaggio. Their nearest challengers are the St. Louis Cardinals from the National League, with eleven wins from nineteen appearances.

PLAYER WITH THE MOST MLS GOALS IN A SEASON

CARLOS VELA

Mexican soccer star Carlos Vela made his name while playing for the Spanish team Real Sociedad, which he joined in 2011. During his time there, he scored seventy-three goals in a six-year, 250-match spell, earning a reputation as one of the most gifted strikers of his generation. In 2017, at age twenty-eight, he turned his back on European football to join Los Angeles FC, where he went on to achieve further glory: During the 2019 season, he made fifteen assists and scored an MLS (Major League Soccer) record thirty-four goals.

MOST MLS GOALS IN A SEASON

Goals	Player	Club, Season
34	Carlos Vela	Los Angeles FC, 2019
31	Josef Martínez	Atlanta United FC, 2018
30	Zlatan Ibrahimović	Los Angeles Galaxy, 2019

WOMEN WITH THE MOST INTERNATIONAL SOCCER CAPS		
Number of caps (career years)		
Kristine Lilly, USA	354	1987-2010
Christine Sinclair, Canada	324	2000-present
Carli Lloyd, USA	316	2005-2021
Christie Pearce, USA	311	1997-2015
Mia Hamm, USA	276	1987-2004

WOMAN WITH THE MOST INTERNATIONAL SOCCER CAPS

KRISTINE LILLY

In her long and successful career, Kristine Lilly played club soccer principally with the Boston Breakers. When she made her debut on the US national team in 1987, however, she was still in high school. Her total of 354 international caps is the world's highest for a man or woman, and her trophy haul includes two World Cup winner's medals and two Olympic golds.

COUNTRY WITH THE MOST FIFA WORLD CUP WINS

BRAZIL

Brazil, host of the 2014 FIFA World Cup, has lifted the trophy the most times in the tournament's history. Germany, second on the list, has more runner-up and semifinal appearances and hence, arguably, a stronger record overall. However, many would say that Brazil's 1970 lineup, led by the incomparable Pelé, ranks as the finest team ever. The host team has won five of the twenty tournaments that have been completed to date.

FIFA WORLD CUP WINNERS
(Number of wins)

Brazil (5)	1958, 1962, 1970, 1994, 2002
Germany* (4)	1954, 1974, 1990, 2014
Italy (4)	1934, 1938, 1982, 2006
Argentina (3)	1978, 1986, 2022
Uruguay (2)	1930, 1950
France (2)	1998, 2018
* As West Germany 1954, 1974	

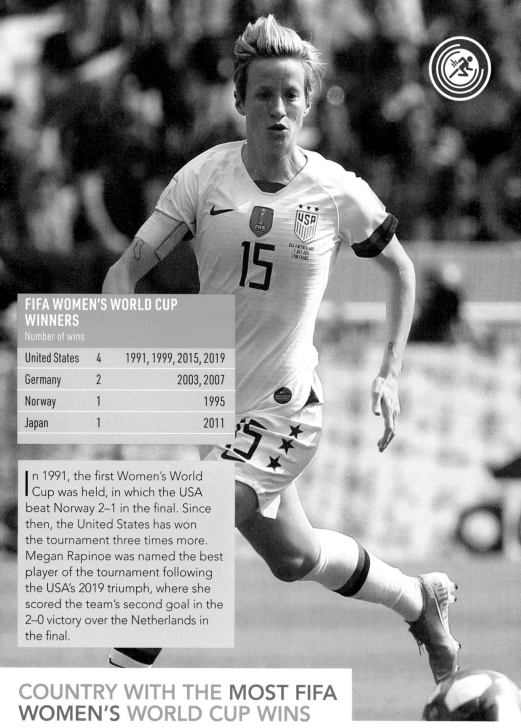

FIFA WOMEN'S WORLD CUP WINNERS
Number of wins

United States	4	1991, 1999, 2015, 2019
Germany	2	2003, 2007
Norway	1	1995
Japan	1	2011

In 1991, the first Women's World Cup was held, in which the USA beat Norway 2–1 in the final. Since then, the United States has won the tournament three times more. Megan Rapinoe was named the best player of the tournament following the USA's 2019 triumph, where she scored the team's second goal in the 2–0 victory over the Netherlands in the final.

COUNTRY WITH THE **MOST FIFA WOMEN'S** WORLD CUP WINS

UNITED STATES

MOST BALLON D'OR WINS
LIONEL MESSI

A skilled playmaker, Argentina's Lionel Messi is considered by many to be the greatest soccer player of his generation. Before moving to Inter Miami in 2023 (following two seasons at Paris Saint-Germain), Messi had spent almost his entire career with Barcelona, his team winning thirty-five trophies. He holds the all-time record for the most La Liga goals (474) and the most international goals by a South American player (ninety-eight). He is also the only player in the game's history to have won the Ballon d'Or, awarded annually since 1956 to the world's best player, on eight occasions (in 2009, 2010, 2011, 2012, 2015, 2019, 2021, and 2023).

FASTEST SCORING SHOT AT THE 2022 FIFA WORLD CUP
KYLIAN MBAPPÉ

With France trailing 2–0 in the 2022 FIFA World Cup final against Argentina, their star player Kylian Mbappé managed to drag his team back into the game. First, in the eightieth minute, he converted a penalty; ninety-seven seconds later, he made a stunning strike from the edge of the penalty area—clocked at 76.67 mph, it was the fastest scoring shot recorded at the tournament. The star scored from the spot again in extra time to become only the second player in history to net a hat trick in a FIFA World Cup final (after England's Geoff Hurst in 1966). But his World Cup final dream ended in disappointment; Argentina went on to win the penalty shoot-out 4–2 to lift the trophy for the third time.

SERENA WILLIAMS

Serena Williams is truly one of the all-time greats in tennis, playing with a combination of power and athleticism that has made her almost unbeatable when she's been at her best. Williams first won a Grand Slam singles title at the US Open in 1999 and has since added five more, plus three in France and seven each in Australia and at Wimbledon. She's tough to beat in doubles, too. She and her sister Venus Williams have reached fourteen Grand Slam finals together—and won them all.

SERENA WILLIAMS GRAND SLAMS
Finals wins

US Open	1999, 2002, 2008, 2012, 2013, 2014
Australian Open	2003, 2005, 2007, 2009, 2010, 2015, 2017
French Open	2002, 2013, 2015
Wimbledon	2002, 2003, 2009, 2010, 2012, 2015, 2016

Serbian Novak Djokovic is the world's most successful tennis player. Turning pro in 2003, he recorded one of the greatest seasons in tennis history in 2011, winning seventy of seventy-six matches and claiming the Australian Open, Wimbledon, and US Open titles. He has gone on to win eight further Australian Open titles, three French Open titles, six Wimbledon crowns, and another three US Open titles. His haul of twenty-four Grand Slam titles is the most by any male tennis player ever.

MALE PLAYER WITH MOST GRAND SLAM VICTORIES
NOVAK DJOKOVIC

GRAND SLAM TITLES	PLAYERS	AUSTRALIAN OPEN	FRENCH OPEN	WIMBLEDON	US OPEN
24	Novak Djokovic (Serbia, 2008–)	10	3	7	4
22	Rafael Nadal (Spain, 2005–)	2	14	2	4
20	Roger Federer (Switzerland, 2003–2018)	6	1	8	5

NHL TEAM WITH THE
MOST STANLEY CUP WINS
MONTREAL CANADIENS

STANLEY CUP WINNERS (SINCE 1915)		
Number of wins (time span)		
Montreal Canadiens	24	1916-1993
Toronto Maple Leafs	13	1918-1967
Detroit Red Wings	11	1936-2008
Boston Bruins	6	1929-2011
Chicago Blackhawks	6	1934-2015

The Montreal Canadiens are the oldest and, by far, the most successful National Hockey League team. In its earliest years, the Stanley Cup had various formats, but since 1927, it has been awarded exclusively to the champion NHL team—and the Canadiens have won it roughly one year in every four. Their most successful years were the 1940s through the 1970s, when the team was inspired by all-time greats like Maurice Richard and Guy Lafleur.

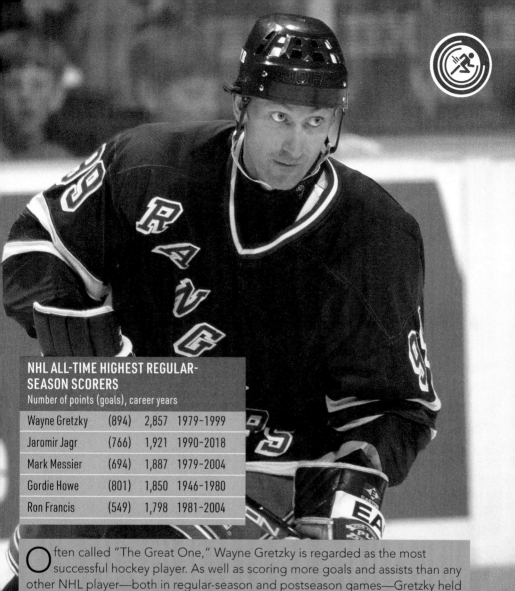

NHL ALL-TIME HIGHEST REGULAR-SEASON SCORERS

Number of points (goals), career years

Wayne Gretzky	(894)	2,857	1979–1999
Jaromir Jagr	(766)	1,921	1990–2018
Mark Messier	(694)	1,887	1979–2004
Gordie Howe	(801)	1,850	1946–1980
Ron Francis	(549)	1,798	1981–2004

Often called "The Great One," Wayne Gretzky is regarded as the most successful hockey player. As well as scoring more goals and assists than any other NHL player—both in regular-season and postseason games—Gretzky held over sixty NHL records in all by the time of his retirement in 1999. The majority of these records still stand. Although he was unusually small for an NHL player, Gretzky had great skills and an uncanny ability to be in the right place at the right time.

NHL PLAYER WITH THE
MOST CAREER POINTS

WAYNE GRETZKY

MANON

FIRST WOMAN TO PLAY IN AN NHL GAME

RHÉAUME

Manon Rhéaume had a fine career as a goaltender in women's ice hockey, earning World Championship gold medals with the Canadian National Women's Team. She is also the first—and only—woman to play for an NHL club. On September 23, 1992, she played one period for the Tampa Bay Lightning in an exhibition game against the St. Louis Blues, during which she saved seven of nine shots. She later played twenty-four games for various men's teams in the professional International Hockey League.

The NASCAR drivers' championship has been contested since 1949. California native Jimmie Johnson is tied at the top of the all-time wins list with seven, but his five-season streak, 2006–2010, is easily the best in the sport's history. Johnson's racing career began on 50cc motorcycles when he was five years old. All of his NASCAR championship wins were achieved driving Chevrolets. He won eighty-three NASCAR races in his career, the last in 2017. He retired from NASCAR in 2020 but still competes in IndyCar events.

NASCAR CHAMPIONSHIP WINS
Number of wins (years in which the title was won)

Jimmie Johnson	7	2006, 2007, 2008, 2009, 2010, 2013, 2016
Dale Earnhardt, Sr.	7	1980, 1986, 1987, 1990, 1991, 1993, 1994
Richard Petty	7	1964, 1967, 1971, 1972, 1974, 1975, 1979
Jeff Gordon	4	1995, 1997, 1998, 2001

MOST CONSECUTIVE NASCAR CHAMPIONSHIP WINS
JIMMIE JOHNSON

ALL-TIME MOST SUCCESSFUL FEMALE SNOWBOARD CROSS COMPETITOR

LINDSEY JACOBELLIS

JACOBELLIS'S MEDAL TALLY

Olympics	2 golds, 1 silver
World Championships	6 golds, 1 bronze
Winter X Games	10 golds, 1 silver, 1 bronze

Snowboard cross races were only invented in the 1990s, and for much of their history since then, Lindsey Jacobellis has been the dominant female athlete in the event. Coming up to the 2022 Winter Olympics, Jacobellis had won six World Championships and taken gold ten times at the Winter X Games, but her best Olympic performance, in four attempts, had been a silver in 2006, when she blew a winning lead by celebrating before she crossed the finish line. She finally got it right in Beijing, though, taking two golds for Team USA, in the individual event and the mixed team.

Erin Jackson gained her first big sporting successes as an in-line speed skater and in roller derby. Jackson was an in-line-skating medalist in the 2015 Pan-American Games, and it was only in 2016 that she switched to speed skating on ice. She lacked experience at her first Olympics in 2018 but did everything right in Beijing in 2022. Her winning time of 37.04 seconds in the 500-meter race gave her a 0.08-second margin of victory. There are two types of indoor ice-skating races. Long-track races in international competitions take place on a 400-meter circuit, similar in size to a standard running track. Short-track races take place on a circuit created on an international-size hockey rink. The long-track races are faster, but the short-track ones can be very dramatic, with many crashes and falls.

FIRST BLACK WOMAN TO WIN AN INDIVIDUAL WINTER OLYMPIC GOLD MEDAL

ERIN JACKSON

NATHAN CHEN

FIRST-EVER SKATER TO LAND SIX QUADRUPLE JUMPS

Nathan Chen made skating history at the 2018 Winter Olympics by being the first-ever skater to attempt and land six quadruple jumps during one performance. Quad jumps—in which the skater spins around four times while in the air—are among the hardest moves in skating, and grouping several of them in one program makes them more difficult still. Chen's record-breaking moves did not win a medal, because he skated poorly in another part of the competition, but he won the 2018 World Championship after landing his six quads once again. He retained his title in 2019 and added a third world gold in 2021. Chen finally won Olympic gold at Beijing in 2022 in the men's singles competition, though this time attempting "only" five quad jumps in his free skate program.

A professional skateboarder, successful musician, and Olympic and X Games star, Shaun White has an astonishing range of talents. He has won more X Games gold medals than anyone else, but his three Olympic golds, in the half-pipe competitions in 2006, 2010, and 2018, the most ever by a snowboarder, are perhaps his biggest achievement. The best of all was in 2018, when he landed two super-difficult back-to-back tricks in the final round to jump into first place. White's medal happened to be the USA's 100th at the Winter Olympics. White again made the USA Olympic team for Beijing 2022, just missing out on another medal with fourth place in the half-pipe. He announced his retirement from competition after this event.

MOST WINTER OLYMPICS
SNOWBOARDING GOLD MEDALS
SHAUN WHITE

MOST GOLD MEDALS IN WORLD CLIMBING COMPETITIONS
JANJA GARNBRET

Competition climbing has recently become an Olympic sport. Climbers compete on indoor climbing walls in three disciplines—lead climbing, speed climbing, and bouldering—to arrive at a combined score for a medal. Janja Garnbret, who is from Slovenia, has won more gold medals than any other climber, male or female, in World Championships and World Cup events. She has enjoyed huge success at the World Championships, winning eight gold medals (including the combined title in 2018, 2019, and 2023). In 2020, she also won the first-ever women's Olympic gold medal awarded in her sport; the winner of the men's competition in Tokyo was Alberto Ginés López of Spain.

ARMAND

**HIGHEST
POLE VAULT**

DUPLANTIS

B orn in 1999 and raised in Louisiana by an American father and Swedish
mother, Armand "Mondo" Duplantis started setting pole-vault records when
he was still in elementary school. After choosing to compete for his mother's
homeland, he landed his first big win in adult competition in the 2018 European
Athletics Championships. In 2019, he gained a silver medal in the World
Championships, but in 2022 he moved ahead of the field in his event, setting a
new world record of 6.21 meters (20 feet, 4.25 inches). He went even better at
Eugene, Oregon, on September 17, 2023, clearing 6.23 meters (20 feet, 5 inches).

MOST SUCCESSFUL SURFER OF ALL TIME
KELLY SLATER

Born on February 11, 1972, Kelly Slater grew up in Cocoa Beach, Florida, and started surfing at the age of five. By age ten, he was winning age-division events up and down the Atlantic coast and, in 1984, he won his first age-division national title. He turned professional in 1990, won his first pro event—the Rip Curl Pro in France—in 1992, and ended the year by becoming world champion for the first time. He claimed five successive world titles between 1994 and 1998 before taking a break from the sport—only to return in 2002 and earn a further five titles between 2005 and 2011. His haul of eleven World Surf League titles is an all-time record.

MOST DECORATED FEMALE
SWIMMER IN HISTORY
KATIE LEDECKY

At age 15, Katie Ledecky qualified for the US Olympic team for London 2012 and shocked the world by surging to 800-meter freestyle gold. Further success followed at the 2013 World Championships when she took four gold medals, setting the 800m and 1500m world records in the process, and she raced to five more World Championship golds in 2015. She took four gold medals at the 2016 Olympics and her domination of the pool continued with five golds at the 2017 World Championships. Despite suffering from illness, she retained her 800m world title in 2019, and the gold rush continued at the 2020 Olympics (two) and the 2021 World Championships (four). Now with twenty-eight gold medals, she is the most decorated female swimmer in history.

MOST OLYMPIC GOLDS WON BY AN INDIVIDUAL MICHAEL PHELPS

Michael Phelps may be the greatest competitive swimmer ever. He did not win any medals at his first Olympics in 2000, but at each of the Summer Games from 2004 through 2016, he was the most successful individual athlete of any nation. When he announced his retirement after London 2012, he was already the most decorated Olympic athlete ever— but he didn't stay retired for long. At Rio 2016, he won five more golds and a silver, taking his medal total to twenty-eight—twenty-three of them gold.

MOST SUCCESSFUL OLYMPIANS
Number of medals won (gold)

Michael Phelps, USA	Swimming	2004-2016	28 (23)
Larisa Latynina, USSR	Gymnastics	1956-1964	18 (9)
Marit Bjørgen, Norway	Cross-country skiing	2002-2018	15 (8)
Nikolai Andrianov, USSR	Gymnastics	1972-1980	15 (7)

Simone Biles won her first two World Championship titles in 2013 at the age of sixteen and has added to her total every season since then, apart from during a career break in 2017. Biles is only four feet, eight inches tall, but her tiny frame is full of power and grace, displayed most memorably in her favorite floor exercise discipline. She is so good that several special moves are named after her—and they are so difficult that she is the only competitor so far to perform these in championships. To date, she has won four Olympic and twenty-three World Championship gold medals. Biles has also been widely praised as a champion for mental health awareness and for her bravery in speaking out as a victim in an abuse scandal in her sport.

MOST DECORATED GYMNAST EVER
SIMONE BILES

WORLD RECORD HOLDER IN WOMEN'S 400-METER HURDLES SYDNEY MCLAUGHLIN

New Jersey native Sydney McLaughlin triumphed at the 2021 Tokyo Olympics in perhaps the greatest track race of the Games. McLaughlin had set a new world record of 51.90 seconds in the US Olympic trials, edging ahead of her great rival Dalilah Muhammad. Muhammad smashed that mark with 51.58 in the Tokyo final, but McLaughlin stayed in front with an astonishing 51.46 win. She went on to better that mark, clocking a staggering 50.68 seconds in Eugene, Oregon, on July 22, 2022.

FASTEST WOMEN'S 400M HURDLES

Sydney McLaughlin (USA)	50.68	2022
Sydney McLaughlin (USA)	51.41	2022
Sydney McLaughlin (USA)	51.46	2021
Dalilah Muhammad (USA)	51.58	2021
Sydney McLaughlin (USA)	51.61	2022

FASTEST 100M SPRINTS OF ALL TIME
Time in seconds

Usain Bolt (Jamaica)	9.58	Berlin 2009
Usain Bolt (Jamaica)	9.63	London 2012
Usain Bolt (Jamaica)	9.69	Beijing 2008
Tyson Gay (USA)	9.69	Shanghai 2009
Yohan Blake (Jamaica)	9.69	Lausanne 2012

USAIN BOLT

FASTEST MAN IN THE WORLD

Jamaica's top athlete, Usain Bolt, is the greatest track sprinter who has ever lived. Other brilliant Olympic finalists have described how all they can do is watch as Bolt almost disappears into the distance. Usain's greatest victories have been his triple Olympic gold medals at London 2012 and Rio 2016, plus two gold medals from Beijing 2008. Usain also holds the 100-meter world record (9.58s) and the 200-meter record (19.19s), both from the 2009 World Championships.

MOST DECORATED PARALYMPIAN EVER
TRISCHA ZORN

Trischa Zorn is the most successful Paralympian of all time, having won an astonishing fifty-five medals, forty-one of them gold, at the Paralympic Games from 1980 to 2004. She won every Paralympic event she entered from 1980 to 1988. Zorn is blind and helps military veterans with disabilities enter the world of parasport. Zorn was inducted into the Paralympic Hall of Fame in 2012.

LEADING PARALYMPIC MEDALISTS
Number of medals won

Trischa Zorn, USA	55
Heinz Frei, Switzerland	35
Jonas Jacobsson, Sweden	30
Zipora Rubin-Rosenbaum, Israel	30
Jessica Long, USA	29

Although China topped the Paralympic medal table at the 2022 Winter Games in Beijing (61 medals), with the United States coming in fifth (20 medals), the United States comfortably leads the all-time medal count in the Paralympic Summer Games. Norway heads the standings in the Winter Games, with the United States in third place, giving the United States an overall medal total that will be unbeatable for many years to come.

COUNTRIES WITH THE MOST PARALYMPIC MEDALS
Total number of medals won

United States	2,618
Great Britain	1,954
Germany*	1,934
China	1,299
France	1,275

*includes totals of former East and West Germany

COUNTRY WITH THE MOST ALL-TIME PARALYMPIC MEDALS
USA

bottom: AP Photo/Kamran Jebreili; 162: AP Photo/Eric Risberg; 163: Wolfgang Kaehler/Alamy Stock Photo; 166: Operation IceBridge/NASA; 169: Auscape/Universal Images Group via Getty Images; 171: NASA image by Jeff Schmaltz, MODIS Rapid Response Team; 173: Henrique Casinhas/SOPA Images/LightRocket via Getty Images; 176: NASA Earth Observatory images by Jesse Allen; 178: Majdi Fathi/NurPhoto/Shutterstock; 181: Amos Chapple/Shutterstock; 182–183, 234: Edwin Remsberg/VWPics via AP Images; 184 top: Selina Zhang; 184 bottom: Governor's Office/Hal Yeager; 185 top: Bear River State Park; 185 center: Courtesy of Crater of Diamonds State Park; 185 bottom: Minnesota State Emblems Redesign Commission; 186: Dan Anderson via ZUMA Wire/Newscom; 187: Joe Raedle/Getty Images; 190: EuroStyle Graphics/Alamy Stock Photo; 192: Randy Duchaine/Alamy Stock Photo; 193: Prisma by Dukas Presseagentur GmbH/Alamy Stock Photo; 194: BluePlanetArchive/Michael S. Nolan; 196: AP Photo/Lucy Pemoni; 197: Steve Conner/Icon SMI/Corbis via Getty Images; 199: Buyenlarge/Getty Images; 200: Don Smetzer/Alamy Stock Photo; 201: Wolfgang Kaehler/LightRocket via Getty Images; 202: Stephen J. Cohen/Getty Images; 203: John Cancalosi/Pantheon/SuperStock; 208: AP Photo/Aaron Lavinsky/Star Tribune; 209: Richard Finkelstein for the USA IBC; 210: Historic Collection/Alamy Stock Photo; 213: REUTERS/Alamy Stock Photo; 214: Nansen Ski Club; 215: Loop Images/UIG via Getty Images; 216 bottom: Visit Las Cruces; 217: Tina Pomposelli; 218: AP Photo/Alan Marler; 220: Library of Congress; 221: joel zatz/Alamy Stock Photo; 222: Courtesy of Wolferman's Bakery™; 223: AP Photo/Matt Rourke; 224: Jerry Coli/Dreamstime.com; 225: Ed Currie/PuckerButt Pepper Company; 226: Sergio Pitamitz/robertharding/Newscom; 228: Fritz Polking/VWPics/Alamy Stock Photo; 229: Prisma by Dukas Presseagentur GmbH/Alamy Stock Photo; 231: Courtesy of National Park Service, Maggie L. Walker National Historic Site; 235: Richard Maschmeyer/age fotostock/SuperStock; 236–237, 259: AP Photo/Frank Franklin II; 238 top: Khalid Alhaj/MB Media/Getty Images; 238 bottom: Kevin Mazur/WireImage/Getty Images; 239 top: AP Photo/Rebecca Blackwell; 239 center: Bruce Yeung/Getty Images; 239 bottom: Jan Kruger/Getty Images; 240: Streeter Lecka/Getty Images; 241: Gian Ehrenzeller/EPA/Shutterstock; 242: Tony Donaldson/Icon SMI/Newscom; 243: Stew Milne/AP Images for Hasbro; 244: Ronald Martinez/Getty Images; 245: AP Photo/Elaine Thompson; 246–247: AP Photo/Mark J. Terrill; 248: AP Photo/Greg Trott; 249: ERIK S LESSER/EPA-EFE/Shutterstock; 250: Kevork Djansezian/Getty Images; 251: Jed Jacobsohn/Getty Images; 252: Jevone Moore/CSM/Shutterstock; 253: Guang Niu/Getty Images; 254: AP Photo; 255: AP Photo/David Vincent; 256: AP Photo/Lynne Sladky; 257: Sebastian Frej/MB Media/Getty Images; 258: Adam Pretty/Getty Images; 260: Bruce Bennett Studios/Getty Images; 261: Rocky Widner/Getty Images; 262: Bruce Bennett Studios/Getty Images; 263: Jared C. Tilton/Getty Images; 264: Andrew Milligan/PA Images via Getty Images; 265: The World of Sports SC/Shutterstock; 266: MARCO BERTORELLO/AFP/Getty Images; 267: The Yomiuri Shimbun via AP Images; 268: Aflo Co. Ltd./Alamy Stock Photo; 269: Oleksiewicz/PressFocus/Shutterstock; 270: Koji Hirano/Getty Images; 271: Tom Pennington/Getty Images; 272: Mitchell Gunn/Dreamstime.com; 273: Robert Gauthier/Los Angeles Times via Getty Images; 274: AP Photo/Morry Gash; 275: Stuart Robinson/Express Newspapers via AP Images; 276: ARIS MESSINIS/AFP/Getty Images; 277: Raphael Dias/Getty Images; 288: News Licensing/MEGA TheMegaAgency.com/Newscom. All other photos © Getty Images and Shutterstock.com.

THE LAST WORD
BEST CHARITY FUNDRAISER
MAX WOOSEY

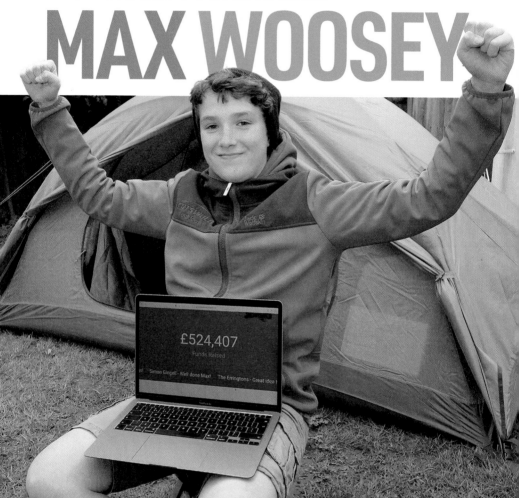

£524,407
Funds Raised

Simon Gingell - Well done Max!   The Erringtons - Great idea

In 2020, Max Woosey's neighbor Rick Abbott gave him a tent and told him to "go have an adventure." Living in Devon, England, Max was just ten years old at the time, and his neighbor was sick with cancer. Max was so inspired by the gift, and so touched by the care his neighbor was receiving at North Devon Hospice, that he decided to sleep in the tent every night. For the next three years, he camped in his backyard to raise money for the charity. After raising $790,000 for the hospice, Max finally spent his last night camping out on April 1, 2023. He had turned that one adventure into many and received several awards for his efforts, among them a British Empire Medal.